W9-BMU-000

Emotional management is a vital life skill to learn. It is such a challenge for most people to maintain an even emotional keel throughout the course of life. Often, the imbalance becomes great enough to be called depression. Transforming Depression *is an excellent tool. It presents a wonderful mix of compassion, science and personal stories to teach emotional management techniques that are easy and backed by hard science. We as care providers should read this book to better understand ourselves and our patients. Patients should use this book as an extension of therapy, reviewing it as they stretch and grow out of the darkness. It's not just another self help book!*

> —Wendy Warner, MD, FACOG, president of the American Board of Holistic Medicine and founder and medical director of Medicine In Balance, LLC

Using the HeartMath tools in conjunction with the emWave technology has offered a sense of relief for Duke Medicine's oncology inpatient population. Patients have reported not only a reduction in their amount of perceived stress, but an overall lifestyle change has been achieved. They have learned to change the way they view their stressors, resulting in a reduction of depression symptomatology. HeartMath tools are the only ones I have used that continue to assist the patients long after their discharge—a gift that keeps on giving.

> —Kristy L Everette, LRT/CTRS, oncology recreation therapy coordinator at the Duke Comprehensive Cancer Center at the Duke University Medical Center

I love the profound work that HeartMath is doing and I'm grateful for their important contributions to society. They have identified the real power of the heart. Transforming Depression *is very effective—it helps people remove the blocks they couldn't address before and bring more peace to their lives.*

> —Marci Shimoff, author of *Happy for No Reason* and coauthor of *Chicken Soup for the Woman's Soul*

HeartMath's potential for healing mental health issues continues to amaze me! After many years of using HeartMath in my psychotherapy practice, the tools in this book continue to prove extremely effective in working with struggling and depressed youth, many of whom are living in dire situations. My clients have demonstrated an overall improvement in functioning, and a sharp decrease in depression symptoms. Best of all, my clients are in charge of the process of transformation and they use HeartMath's skills every day in their lives no matter what their life circumstances are!

> —Steve Sawyer, LCSW, SAC, CCS, APSW, CSIT, licensed psychotherapist and substance abuse counselor

This HeartMath solution is very effective for treating depression. By learning how to focus on the heart and perceive more from the heart, patients with depression see the possibility of how to change their feeling and thinking—the core of their problem. This is a very useful book for both patients and professionals.

> —Charly Cungi, MD, physician in private practice in Rumilly, France

In my many years of teaching physicians, nurses and patients how to manage their emotions, I have found no tools more effective than HeartMath. As depression has a significant impact on health, everyone should pay attention to this book.

> —Lee Lipsenthal, MD, ABHM, former medical director of the Ornish Heart Program and founder of Finding Balance in a Medical Life

Childre and Rozman provide a remarkably clear and succinct explanation for the growing impact of depression on our mental and physical health. Although their proposed interventions will take practice, the case histories are provocative, their practical advice is invaluable, and the supporting evidence is compelling.

> —Paul B. Hofmann, Dr.P.H., president of Hofmann Healthcare Group and former director of Stanford University Hospital and Clinics and executive vice president and chief operating officer of the Alta Bates Corp.

For a long time, we doctors have known that depressed patients tend to have more heart disease and vice versa. Psychiatrists and other specialists are becoming more and more aware of the necessity to pay attention to this fact in treatment as well as prevention strategies. I find Transforming Depression *a promising approach to self-help for patients with depressed feelings or patients who are under life stress. The focus on heart-related processes can be of high clinical significance.*

> —Dr. Christina M. van der Feltz-Cornelis, psychiatrist and epidemiologist with the Netherlands Institute of Mental Health and Addiction

HeartMath leads the field again in providing an approach to depression that guides us beyond the conventional, reductionistic, neurobiological approach (anti-depressant medication). Transforming Depression *provides options that work with the body (and mind and spirit) in assisting people to identify and engage in powerful self-regulation skills to re-balance the body and autonomic nervous system, re-connect with heart and spirit, and re-establish a natural state of happiness and health. I recommend it highly!*

> —*Timothy Culbert, MD, FAAP, developmental/behavioral pediatrician and medical* director of the Integrative Medicine Program of the Children's Hospitals and Clinics of Minnesota

Childre, Rozman and the researchers at Heartmath continue to be at the forefront of our understanding of the power of the body to heal the mind. In twenty-three years of treating thousands of patients with anxiety and depression I have yet to encounter a more powerful and user friendly technology. Psychology and psychiatry owe a debt of thanks to Heartmath for helping us find a path through the challenges of today's world.

> —Christian R. Komor, Psy.D., founder of the OCD Recovery Centers of America and author of *The Power of Being*

Heartmath is a refreshing alternative to the prevailing view that to get free of depression we must either take medication or talk (and talk, and talk!) our way out of it. My clients in many countries report that Heartmath offers valuable tools for clearing current depression and other negative emotions as they come up. They use these tools as stand-alone self-help practices, and also to optimize the effect of innovative trauma-based treatments such as EMDR and the energy psychotherapies.

—John Hartung, Psy.D., codirector of the Bodymind Integration Institute of Singapore and author of *Reaching Further*

Transforming Depression *is an effective easy-to-read book explaining the effects of stress on health. It eloquently presents the highly effective HeartMath techniques to achieve heart/brain coherence in a way that can be easily applied by all. Definitely a worthwhile read!*

—Eric I. Hassid, MD, medical director of the Institute for Restorative Health, board certified in neurology by the American Board of Psychiatry and Neurology, and member of the American Academy of Neurology

Transforming Depression

The HeartMath® Solution to Feeling Overwhelmed, Sad, and Stressed

Doc Childre • Deborah Rozman, Ph.D.

New Harbinger Publications, Inc.

Publisher's Note

This publication is designed to provide accurate and authoritative information in regard to the subject matter covered. It is sold with the understanding that the publisher is not engaged in rendering psychological, financial, legal, or other professional services. If expert assistance or counseling is needed, the services of a competent professional should be sought.

HeartMath, Heart Lock-In, and Cut-Thru are registered trademarks of the Institute of HeartMath. Quick Coherence and emWave are registered trademarks of Quantum Intech, Inc. Notice and Ease, Power of Neutral, and Attitude Breathing are registered trademarks of Doc Childre.

Distributed in Canada by Raincoast Books

Copyright © 2007 by Doc Childre and Deborah Rozman
New Harbinger Publications, Inc.
5674 Shattuck Avenue
Oakland, CA 94609
www.newharbinger.com

All Rights Reserved
Printed in the United States of America

Acquired by Catharine Sutker; Cover design by Amy Shoup; Edited by Elisabeth Beller

Library of Congress Cataloging-in-Publication Data

Childre, Doc Lew, 1945-
  Transforming depression : the Heartmath solution to feeling overwhelmed, sad, and stressed / Doc Childre and Deborah Rozman.
     p. cm.
  ISBN-13: 978-1-57224-491-7
  ISBN-10: 1-57224-491-7
  1. Depression, Mental--Popular works. 2. Stress management--Popular works. I. Rozman, Deborah. II. Title.
  RC537.C467 2007
  362.2'5--dc22

                          2007023354

10 09 08
10 9 8 7 6 5 4 3

This book is written with care and compassion, and is dedicated to anyone who is feeling hopeless, sad, and overwhelmed. Know that you are not alone. There literally are millions who feel as you do. Our message is that you don't have to resign yourself to a view that things are not going to get better. The world is going through a period of rapid systemic change and uncertainty. When change is happening faster than you can keep pace, it tends to cause overload and fear, and then the heart shuts down. Depression is an understandable result. It's hard to see light around any corner. Learning how to reopen your heart reconnects you with your spirit and can create new hope and possibilities where none seemed to exist. Our purpose is to provide you with tools and a step-by-step understanding of how to reconnect with your spirit to regain hope and inner peace. Many have done this, and it is our hope that this book will facilitate you as well.

Contents

Foreword

The words "transformation" and "depression" make an apt title for this book, because they have major implications for redemption from depression. It is my belief that depression, like most natural reactions, has some purpose for occurring. It may be the only avenue by which some of us can grow into a greater destiny. Depression may accompany the growth that can come from sad situations, and it may also occur when we discover that the world does not meet our expectations. We become depressed when we see the world as unfair.

Some of the time depression spurs us to action and change within ourselves. Just when we feel most isolated, we have to learn to discover the hidden strengths within ourselves. The personal journeys that take us above the paralysis of depression are often the most courageous events in a lifetime. They reveal the enormous capacities of the human spirit to embrace the power of transformation in the face of long odds and even to relish that challenge. By these acts of renovation of the soul, individuals actually become stronger.

Right now, you may have a hard time imagining how depression can be a transformative experience. Most likely, when you are depressed, you really don't want to do anything. You have no energy to change the channels on the television and might even prefer to sit in darkness than to deal with the disturbances of noises and lights reflecting off the screen. You recognize that your friends and loved ones really are worried about you, and you might even attempt to humor them with a fake smile or make some effort to do something with them. But these activities take some effort, and usually you can't wait for them to end.

What are the resources that can enable a person to emerge from the grips of depression? What accounts for the strengths and resiliency a person finds when depression is resolved? That is the purpose of this book: to give you skills so that depression can be understood as a transformational experience and not as a destructive disease that conquers the spirit. These are the critical steps that can actually infuse you with optimism and joy. Not only are the methods described based on long-standing research, but they are available for everyone to use.

I have worked with depressed children as young as three and with depressed seniors as old as ninety-three, and these approaches are effective. And because they are heart-based, they are something all of us can share. There are hundreds of individuals whose life stories show how they have risen to their destinies as contributors to other lives.

The paths suggested in this book are like journeys to knowing yourself and, most important, are things you can do for yourself. It is time to act. You have the right to be happy and peaceful, but in order to claim that right, you have to make a move. Make a promise to yourself that you will start today.

—G. Frank Lawlis, Ph.D.

Acknowledgments

We want to acknowledge the many people who have lifted themselves out of the depths of resignation, hopelessness, sadness, or despair by putting the concepts and tools in this book into action in their lives. Their success is evidence that people don't have to be mentally and emotionally bound by genetics, traumatic experiences, family upbringing, or societal influence. They have unleashed the transformative power of the heart and, by example, are providing hope to others that they can do the same.

We also acknowledge the HeartMath staff, and the doctors, psychiatrists, psychologists, counselors, and coaches who are dedicated to using the HeartMath System with their clients. We appreciate Dr. Frank Lawlis for writing the foreword to this book and for his pioneering work with the Dr. Phil Show to demystify mental and emotional challenges that affect us all (or people we care about) at some point in our lives.

We also thank Matt McKay, Catharine Sutker, and others at New Harbinger Publications; Dr. Rollin McCraty, director of research at the Institute of HeartMath; our reference editor Dana Tomasino at the Institute of HeartMath; our developmental editor Donna Beech; and our copyeditor Elisabeth Beller. Thank you all for your care and contribution to this work.

Introduction

Everyone feels depressive symptoms from time to time. But these days, more and more people are suffering from a *low-grade depression* that hangs on. Their day-to-day lives are made heavy from overwhelming, sad, anxious, or empty moods. Many people don't even realize they are depressed because they're so used to feeling this way. They think depression is something more extreme than the sense of resignation or hopelessness they feel.

The dictionary describes depression as

feeling pressed down, sad, gloomy, lower in spirits, dispirited;
a condition of general emotional dejection and withdrawal;
sadness greater and more prolonged than that warranted by
any objective reason; a low state of functional activity.

When these feelings are ongoing, they can result in fatigue and loss of energy, problems with sleep, irritability and anxiety, poor concentration, difficulty making decisions, loss of pleasure or interest in daily activities, weight gain or loss, and problems in relationship communications.

It's important to realize that it's normal for healthy people to have these feelings and experiences at different times. But if these moods occur together and often, it has crossed over into a low-grade or a major depression. This book will show anyone how to reduce the length and recurrence of these moods.

A Growing Epidemic of Low-Grade Depression

Depression is now a leading cause of disability worldwide. Experts predict that by 2020, depression will be second only to heart disease as the most disabling condition in the world (Murray and Lopez 1996). Rates of depression have been doubling every ten years—especially in affluent countries. This trend has implications for physical health as well since depressed people have a much greater risk for other illnesses, including cognitive decline, cancer, and heart disease. A long-term study of 1,200 male medical students at Johns Hopkins School of Medicine found that those who experienced depression in school were twice as likely to develop heart disease fifteen years later (Ford et al. 1998). Clinical depression is also present in one of five people with coronary heart disease and in one of three with heart failure (Whooley 2006).

The link between depression and heart disease is not a coincidence. Depression is a "dis-ease" of *heart*, of emotions associated with heart. Of course, biological factors can contribute to depression. But depression is most often caused by an accumulation of unresolved stress and emotional issues that have tilted the body's biochemistry into a state of temporary or chronic imbalance. Unreleased minor and major issues that loom within the subconscious create an emotional *funk* in the feeling world. Sometimes the funk is subtle. At other times, it's obvious. As these feelings fluctuate within the emotional system they hinder your capacity to feel connected to your real self. This, in turn, makes it harder for you to connect with others or experience quality and resonance in relationships.

The accumulation of stress overload that many people are experiencing in today's world is contributing to a growing epidemic of anxiety and depression. As the speed of change in the world ramps up, time demands and pressures at work and in relationships intensify as well. Many people are struggling to keep up, trying to make sense of what's going on in the world and in their own stressful lives. The strain becomes a constant burden that eventually turns into a chronic state of low-grade depression.

Stress and Depression

The ventral right prefrontal cortex of the brain, associated with negative emotions and depression, appears to play a central role in how people respond to stress. Unlike many other brain areas, this part of the prefrontal cortex remains active long after the stressful situation is gone (Wang et al. 2005). So you can't just say, "Now, I'm going to turn the stress off." The prefrontal cortex as a whole is involved in planning, predicting, and forming abstract concepts, and stress overload can continue to negatively impact those functions.

People who suffer from depression also tend to have elevated levels of the stress hormones cortisol and noradrenaline. Too much cortisol can lead to memory and learning problems, brain cell destruction, and depression (Kerr et al. 1991).

When Harvard researchers exposed mice to a corticoid stress hormone for more than two weeks, the mice took significantly longer to emerge from their small dark compartments into a brightly lit open space than they had before exposure. (This is a classic indication of anxiety in animals.) They appeared more fearful and less willing to explore a new environment (Ardayfio and Kim 2006).

Another study found an exaggerated inflammatory response to stress in men with major depression. This may help explain why conditions such as heart disease, cancer, and diabetes often go hand in hand with depression. The study's authors suggest that the increased inflammatory response seen in depressed patients could be due to changes in increased sympathetic nervous system responses and altered cortisol regulation (Pace et al. 2006).

Depression and Heart Health

The HeartMath tools in this book help bring the autonomic nervous system into a healthier state of increased balance and synchronization. Your *autonomic nervous system* (including both sympathetic and parasympathetic nervous systems, discussed in chapter 4) controls 90 percent of your body's involuntary functions. Because your autonomic nervous system is responsible for regulating your hormonal system, immune system, digestion, elimination, sleep, and just about everything that automatically happens with your glands and organs, a healthy functioning autonomic nervous system is absolutely vital to your health and well-being.

Much of the research underlying the HeartMath tools and techniques measures *heart rate variability* (HRV) since it is such an important indicator of autonomic nervous system function. When people become depressed, they begin to feel their world closing in. As things begin to overwhelm them, they feel less flexible and adaptable. Their hearts undergo the same experience. "Reduced HRV" is the term for a heart rate pattern or heart rhythm pattern that does not have the flexibility and adaptability it once had. HeartMath research shows that a healthy HRV can be restored and many types of depression lifted through the use of HeartMath tools.

Medical Costs of Depression and Stress

The Health Enhancement Research Organization (HERO) conducted a three-year health-risk and medical-cost study with 46,000 people from twenty-two companies and government organizations (Goetzel et al. 1998). The study showed that people who reported persistent depression had 70 percent greater medical costs than those who reported not being depressed.

After depression, uncontrolled stress resulted in the second greatest medical costs. Almost 20 percent of the people reported that their stress felt uncontrollable. Their annual medical expenses were 46 percent higher than those of people who were not stressed. Stress was also found to be a significant predictor of cardiovascular disease in women, which is the number one killer of women. Stress contributed to 7.9 percent of cardiovascular disease costs—more than smoking or obesity!

Overall, the people who were both depressed and stressed had medical expenses 147 percent higher than others. This figure is radically higher than the health hazards we hear about more often, such as lack of exercise, smoking, and high blood pressure. In comparison, the increase in medical costs for those health hazards was minor. A sedentary lifestyle resulted in a 10 percent increase in health costs; smoking cost 14 percent more than nonsmoking; and high blood pressure cost 12 percent more. The cost of depression and stress was more than ten times greater than each of these other factors.

HeartMath Interventions

HeartMath biomedical research and studies conducted in hospitals, major corporations, and governmental agencies indicate that emotional states, stress levels, and many chronic diseases can be significantly improved and a lower-risk profile sustained through use of HeartMath tools and techniques (for example, Barrios-Choplin, McCraty, and Cryer 1997; Luskin et al. 2002; McCraty, Atkinson, and Tomasino 2003; for a listing of research studies on the tools of the HeartMath System, see www.heartmath.org/research/research-publications.html).

HeartMath tools give you the capacity to empower yourself. In this book, we use the term "empowerment" to describe mental and emotional self-management in the midst of stress. This power gives you the capacity to become more aligned with the truth in your own heart. Heart empowerment leads to a transformation in your perceptions, mood, and health.

Heart empowerment does not exclude a higher power that is within anyone's belief system. It actually brings people closer to their spiritual source through a process of personal management and connection with the heart.

When people are overloaded with stress, it's hard to connect with anything or anyone, whatever they believe in. This alone can lead to depression. In many cases, depression has resulted from people's hearts trying to tell them something when they weren't listening. Learning how to manage your emotions in the midst of stress makes it easier for you to be in alignment with your deeper heart and spirit.

The Heart and Spirit Connection

Almost every recorded culture and religion has referenced spirit as a source of power, love, and intelligence. But the different ways that people and religions interpret "spirit" have spawned overidentification with and "overattachment" to their interpretations, leading to ongoing separation, conflicts, and wars.

Spirit connects to the body through the heart, mind, emotions, and cells. But it's through the heart that people find their main trunk line for their individual connection to spirit. This is because more spirit comes in through *core heart feelings* of love, care, appreciation, kindness, and compassion. As we'll be discussing in chapters 4 and 5, the heart is designed to receive and generate core heart feelings, which benefit health and well-being and relationships. Core heart feelings draw in *heart intuition*—what people call the "still, small voice" of the heart. HeartMath tools help people reconnect with their core heart feelings and intuitive heart intelligence.

More than ever before, humanity is ready to understand the role of the heart in emotional dynamics and behavioral change. It's through the heart that people evoke the meaningful intent that is needed to transform depression.

When we say "meaningful intent," we don't imply just willpower or mental effort. People can't just turn emotions around with the mind or clear deeply ingrained feelings or beliefs that haunt them from incidents in the past. That type of transformation takes another power of intent that has to be drawn from the heart.

You can't pray, affirm, talk, or rationalize feelings and beliefs away. You have to restore your missing connection with your heart. As you practice the HeartMath tools for emotional management, you will experience reduced stress, more heart intelligence, greater flexibility, and more spirit.

One of the main purposes of emotions in nature's design is to provide a means of expression for uplifting qualities of spirit, like love, compassion, appreciation, kindness, and joy. But because heart intelligence isn't highly developed in most people, the mind's overidentifications and beliefs more often direct emotional energy to be expressed in frustration, blame, anxiety, and depression.

To unfold heart intelligence, people have to take responsibility for their emotional energy management. Until the emotions are regulated, even the most helpful insights cannot be translated through the nervous system and integrated into people's attitudes and lives. That is why regulating one's emotional nature is the next frontier for transforming depression in these fast-paced times. In this book, we will give you a step-by-step process to do this.

chapter 1

Emotional Awareness: The Next Frontier

For the vast majority of people, living is *feeling*. Imagine spending time with a loved one, or sitting in a beautiful spot in nature, or listening to your favorite music, or watching an exciting sports game without any connection whatsoever to your emotional experience. Feelings allow you to experience the textures of life. They are such a natural part of human existence that people often take them for granted.

A life without feeling is a terribly empty place. In fact, when your feelings are numb or suppressed, you're just surviving in a mechanical way. That's why they call it "going through the motions" when someone is shut down emotionally. With no emotion to fuel your actions, everything feels pointless and without meaning. Young or old, people shut down feeling as a defense mechanism when emotional distress becomes too much. *Not feeling* often seems the least painful alternative. When you don't understand the purpose of feelings or how to interpret them, life can become very confusing. You may get stressed, angry, anxious, sad, and then overreact with judgment and blame toward yourself or others. You may end up feeling shut off from people and choosing to withdraw into loneliness.

When anxiety or sadness is ongoing, it builds a state of emotional density that filters out some of your normal textures in life—the sparkle you feel with family or friends, your enjoyment of nature, the moments of inspiration, and the satisfaction you get from your daily activities. Eventually, anxiety or sadness can significantly diminish your rewarding experiences and lead to a chronic feeling of dullness. Depression sets in as your emotional connection to others is gradually reduced to a flat line—a dead zone, without any feeling of purpose or meaning. For some, depression plunges them into a dark hole of despair.

Understanding Depression

Have you ever thought about the word "depression"? It implies something pressing down on you emotionally. No wonder this creates sadness, difficulty in thinking and concentrating, and feelings of dejection and hopelessness. These are all symptoms of depression that cause a lowering of vitality and functional activity. Before long, fatigue sets in.

Depression has many contributing factors. A number of physical conditions can make you more vulnerable to depression. Some people have a genetic predisposition toward pessimism and sadness. Depression can be brought on by hormonal, neurological, or other physical changes. Serious medical conditions like chronic pain, heart disease, cancer, or HIV can also contribute to depression, partly because of the emotional stress they evoke. In other cases, depression is caused by the drugs used to treat medical conditions. Ultimately, depression can make health conditions worse since it weakens the immune system and can make pain harder to bear.

Dramatic global changes are happening today at a faster rate than ever before in human history. The speed of these changes is contributing to the largest rise in numbers of people experiencing depression today. Many people feel so much pressure and anxiety about the future that it puts them in a state of overload. When your emotions can't keep up with everything, your emotional system jams up and then signs off in resignation. When you sign off on your creative life force, it quickly results in depression and a host of other ailments.

Ongoing depression causes biochemical and neurological imbalances that affect the way you feel about yourself and the way you think about things. A state of *dis-ease* keeps stress signals turned on between your heart and brain, which alters the neurotransmitters and hormones getting released in your body, affecting your perceptions and moods. If those stress signals and neurochemical changes become continuous, your brain thinks this is your new normal state and resets itself to *lock in* the pattern. Then no matter what you do, it's hard to feel better. You may suffer silently; reach for solace from friends, religion, or self-help methods; or try therapy or medications. You may bury your distress with overwork or stimulants. But the depression won't release—until you *set a new pattern*.

Three Types of Depression

Doctors have classified three types of depression: major depression, bipolar disorder, and low-level depression (or dysthymia).

If you feel that you are in a dark hole and can't see your way out or if you find yourself caught up in frequent crying spells or suicidal thoughts, you are suffering from major depression. It's important that you see a qualified medical professional to get help immediately. If you are having suicidal thoughts, call your local crisis hotline or 911 and ask them to direct you to that hotline.

If you have bipolar disorder—indicated by wildly swinging mood changes, from manic to depressive states—it's also important that you seek medical treatment.

If you don't know where to go for help, call your local mental health center or visit the National Institute of Mental Health website at www.nimh.nih.gov.

If you are reading this book because a family member or friend is depressed, it's important that you encourage him or her to see a competent medical professional to determine the type of depression and treatment needed. This book can help you better understand your friend or loved one. It's written to be an adjunct treatment for depression.

We have tremendous compassion for those suffering from major depression or bipolar disorder. The main purpose of this book, however, is to help people recover from and prevent the most common type of depression—known as low-level depression. If it goes untreated, it can turn into a major depression.

Low-Level Depression

Many people either don't recognize or won't admit that they have an ongoing, low-level depression. They may believe they are just pessimistic—thinking that life isn't going to get better. Particularly if they have grown up around depressive people, they may think that being down in the dumps much of the time is normal or just part of their personality. This is not the case.

Low-level depression is characterized by frequent down moods and confusing thoughts. It isn't just a passing bleak mood. You may find yourself always negatively projecting the worst outcomes and believing your own thoughts, constantly brooding about what you could or should have done, then feeling bad or guilty that you didn't. You may even think you're going crazy.

Low-level depression is not something you can just pull yourself out of with positive thinking. These mental and emotional attitudes—along with their accompanying biochemical and neurological imbalances—took time to build up. It will also take some time to bring them back to balance. But it doesn't have to take as long as it feels like it will take.

That's the hope of this book. New scientific research along with a new understanding of how emotional energy works shows that you *can* transform depression. New tools are available to help you reconnect with the positive, regenerating textures of life and regain the hope and clarity you have lost.

Allison is living proof of this. Here's what she wrote:

> *Last spring, before I started using the new HeartMath tools, I felt sad, depressed, confused, and defeated most of the time. I could not truly enjoy my daughter or my fiancé or the good in life. It felt like it was only a matter of time before everything would come crumbling down.*
>
> *After I started using the HeartMath tools, I realized I was no longer a victim. It wasn't some sort of magic pill that made things better all at once, but practicing the tools ignited something like a magic flame burning inside of me. The more I look at it, the stronger it gets. And the most wonderful thing about it is—it's mine. No one but me truly controls it.*
>
> *I could go on and on about how these tools have changed my life. I have become the mother, wife, and person I have always wanted to be. I am so grateful to be one of the ones who got to learn them. After seeing what a difference HeartMath has made in my life, I believe it is something every person needs. It is truly the greatest gift of information I have ever received.*

What You Will Learn in This Book

Our goal in *Transforming Depression* is to provide you with a scientifically validated and user-friendly system to release and prevent depression. The book provides information and powerful yet simple tools and exercises to keep you from repeating downward spirals. It explains some of the breakthrough research behind the HeartMath tools and offers case studies from health professionals and individuals who have successfully used these tools to lift depression. To transform emotions is to know how to direct your emotional energy and intentions for better outcomes.

Many of the HeartMath tools and techniques provided in this book are the same or similar to those in the other books in the Transforming series: *Transforming Anger, Transforming Stress,* and *Transforming Anxiety.* They serve the same purpose of *resetting your patterns* and *regridding your emotional response system.* Each book was written for a different application and teaches you how to use the HeartMath tools to transform specific problems, many of which are unique to this time period in history.

Transforming Depression will help you understand the planetary shift that is occurring and how that is contributing to depression for so many. It covers what *you* need to do for emotional energy maintenance so that you don't accumulate overload and anxiety in your system to the point where most of your attitudes take a pessimistic downturn, resulting in loss of interest in life.

Preventive maintenance is exactly what you need in order to release your anxiety and stress overload before they create a buildup that results in low-grade depression. Through the sincere application of the exercises and tools, you *can* lift your attitudes and moods and make things easier. These tools will also help you unfold your intuition to discover what additional help you need or what new directions to take.

Take your time with each chapter. Read and ponder it from the heart, and see how it applies to you. Do the exercises and use the tools before moving on to the next chapter. The first part of the book covers tools to clear stressful feelings as they come up. The second part covers emotional restructuring techniques to release longer-term emotional issues and depressive perspectives. The last part covers deep psychology on the root causes of many depressive patterns and discusses how to use the tools and techniques you've learned in the book to clear them. Take the book to heart, and it will help you develop awareness and understanding to step into a new emotional frontier.

The Next Frontier

If you take a look at the history of humanity, emotional advancement hasn't made much progress since people were living in caves, while intellectual advancement has soared! This isn't an evolutionary mistake. It's all about timing. Now is the time for humanity's developed intellect to learn to understand the most sensitive of human qualities—our *feelings*.

The next frontier of human advancement—personally and collectively—is the emotional frontier. Your task—and the task of humanity—is to learn *how* to intelligently resolve *feelings* for your own and others' benefit, in order to enrich your experience of life and create a better future.

Many people would say that this goal is idealistic for society, even more so for themselves. Hard as they have tried, they can't see beyond their own beliefs, fears, and insecurities. If they are honest about it, their emotional world is often in chaos. Nevertheless, it's emotion that controls their lives, perpetuates their distress, and portends their future.

Most people spend a lot of energy keeping their houses clean, their bills paid, and their workplaces in order. Even if they lead relatively happy lives, they usually also have one or two scenarios that are a constant, nagging source of emotional stress and dissatisfaction that drains their energy. The most common response to these emotions is to push them down or try to ignore them. The trouble is, when emotions are repressed, they don't just go away. They are still inside, waiting to be unleashed. These repressed emotions often rule our perceptions and decisions without our being aware of it.

In this book, you will learn about new scientific discoveries that reveal the power of the heart as a *key* to regulating and clearing emotions. The process of *feeling* a feeling or *experiencing* an emotion is both biochemical and neurological. It involves your heart, brain, and nervous and hormonal systems. We use the words "feeling" and "emotion" interchangeably throughout this book. A combination of feeling sensations, associated mental thoughts, and biochemical reactions shape human beliefs and emotional experience, in gradations from very pleasant to very painful. Feelings of worry, anxiety, hurt, frustration, guilt, fear, sadness, numbness, and depression are usually experienced as uncomfortable or distressing, whereas feelings of love, care, joy, compassion, appreciation, and bliss tend to be uplifting, releasing, and energizing. Uncomfortable feelings keep you focused on yourself and your own interests to try to relieve the distress and pain. Uplifting feelings expand your perception so you can think of the welfare of others as well as your own.

People are more ready than ever to learn how to connect with their own hearts. With humanity's very survival at stake, many are looking deeper into their hearts for answers. They are coming to understand that the heart is where people go when the mind doesn't have an answer. Science is verifying the heart's role in feeling and intuition, at a time when there is a global need for more people to engage their hearts. Learning the language of the heart, the language of one's feeling world, is a next step. It's time for more heart on the planet. As people learn how to manage their emotions from the heart, then a new intelligence and understanding can emerge.

The heart's intelligence and power are seated in love, and the world is more ready than ever to learn about love. Most people feel that the purpose and meaning of life has something to do with love. That's really why they're here—to learn how to love more and love better, and learning this is becoming an obvious imperative. Everyone wants to love, but few of us have been taught how to love or be loved.

Understanding brings hope. If you can learn to understand *the language of the feeling world* at the root of your beliefs and actions, you can better understand how to love and embrace hope for new solutions. The hope of the twenty-first century is that people will recognize that emotions are the next frontier to be understood and managed for personal, social, and planetary peace and quality of life. It starts with you—your own emotional understanding. If you are feeling depressed or have felt depressed in the past, use the Depression Checklist that follows to deepen your understanding of that experience.

If you decided to read this book because you wanted to do something about your depression, then roll up your sleeves and let's get started! You'll learn the most if you keep a notebook or journal to track your progress as you go through the book. It's important to practice the tools and techniques, do the exercises, write down answers to the questions, and make notes about your feelings and perceptions. Make sure, especially, to write down any insights and decisions you make. You will revisit the Depression Checklist later in the book to see how your numbers have changed.

✎ Depression Checklist

Describe your depression. Assign a number on a scale of 0 to 5 to each item, with 0 being "not at all" and 5 being "all the time." Start with Emotional Symptoms and then continue with Mental Symptoms and Physical Symptoms. Make a copy to write on or write in the book so you have a record of your answers.

Emotional Symptoms	Scale of 0 to 5
sadness	_____
moodiness	_____
numbness or dullness	_____
resignation or hopelessness	_____
hopelessness	_____
despair	_____
emptiness	_____
disconnection from others	_____
heartache	_____
resentment	_____
bitterness	_____
guilt	_____
other (describe)	_____
_____	_____

Mental Symptoms	Scale of 0 to 5
self-blame	_____
lack of self-worth	_____

constantly thinking of what's wrong _____

loss of interest in activities _____

confused thoughts _____

difficulty focusing or concentrating _____

difficulty making decisions _____

thinking you're going crazy _____

suicidal thoughts _____

other (describe) _____

_____   _____

Physical Symptoms   **Scale of 0 to 5**

fidgety and restless _____

sleeping too much or too little _____

low energy or fatigued much of the time _____

overeating or loss of appetite _____

no energy for job, chores, or shopping _____

dramatic up and down energy swings _____

  family history of depression _____

other (describe) _____

_____   _____

Note: If you have a lot of 4s and 5s on your checklist—especially on the last few items in any of these categories—it's likely that you are suffering from major depression and need to see a qualified medical professional for help immediately.

chapter 2

The Planetary Shift

In today's world, more people are spiraling down into depression, many at younger ages than ever before. Studies indicate that one out of every ten adults in the United States has a *major* depression in any given year. Many, many more have ongoing, *low-grade* depression. These numbers have been growing steadily. For the past several decades, each successive generation has reported more depressive disorders than the previous one. Today, better recognition of unreported, low-grade, or *subclinical* depression (that is, depression exhibiting fewer than the number of symptoms usually required for clinical diagnosis) is pushing prevalence numbers ever higher (Horwitz and Wakefield 2005).

Women experience depression about twice as often as men (Blehar and Oren 1997). An alarming number of children and teenagers suffer from both major and low-grade depression. Prior to the twenty-first century, depression was rarely seen in young children. Now, children as young as five years old are increasingly diagnosed and treated for depression. Use of antidepressants among youngsters ages five to seventeen tripled from about 2 percent of that population in 1994 to almost 6 percent in 2002 (Bower 2006).

Current Treatments for Depression

The most common medical treatments for depression are psychotherapy and mood-regulating antidepressant drugs—most often selective serotonin reuptake inhibitors (SSRIs), such as Prozac (fluoxetine), Paxil (paroxetine), or Zoloft (sertraline). However, a study by the NIMH found that antidepressant drugs and talk therapy were effective for *only about half* the people with depression. For some, the strong side effects from the drugs weren't worth the benefits they had provided. Other studies have found, surprisingly, that common antidepressants have little more effect than a placebo (sugar pill) (Kirsch et al. 2002; Moncrieff and Kirsch 2005; Moncrieff and Cohen 2006; Raz 2006).

In today's pill-popping culture, many people believe they need to be on antidepressant medication. In England and France, it's estimated that one in five adults takes antidepressants. In 1993, 10.8 million prescriptions for antidepressants were dispensed in the United Kingdom. In 2003, that more than doubled to over 27 million prescriptions written. According to a survey commissioned by the British Association for Counselling and Psychotherapy, *two-thirds* of British adults say they suffer from depression.

Research now suggests that SSRIs, such as Prozac and Seroxat (paroxetine HCL), can be addictive. In 2004, the London water supply was found to be contaminated with unacceptable levels of Prozac from people's sewage systems (Townsend 2004).

Antidepressant drugs are also increasingly prescribed for children, but the safety of such drugs for young people is in question (Bower 2006; Raz 2006). In some cases, antidepressants have been blamed for inciting suicidal tendencies in teens and young adults (Bower 2006; Raz 2006).

There is no question that antidepressants have helped many people to cope better, but these drugs are not enough to cure the root causes of depression. Taking drugs can be like disarming a fire alarm without putting out the fire.

It's the combination of psychotherapy and medication that has proved thus far to be the most effective intervention for major depression. Talk therapies help you get things off your chest, and cognitive behavioral therapy (CBT), the most common intervention, is designed to help you restructure your thoughts and beliefs. However, CBT rarely addresses emotions directly.

Other Treatments

Regular physical exercise can help to temporarily lift moods, but the effect doesn't last if you haven't cleared up unresolved emotional issues. Eventually, those unresolved emotions can weigh you down to the point where exercise doesn't help or you lose the motivation to exercise. There are herbal treatments for depression that have become popular, such as St. John's Wort (*Hypericum perforatum*), although studies are inconclusive as to their benefits. Doctors may prescribe electroshock therapy for people with treatment-resistant major depression. Some depression sufferers have been helped by procedures that were originally designed for use with other medical problems—such as a treatment for epilepsy called vagus-nerve stimulation and a treatment for Parkinson's disease called Area 25 brain stimulation.

Those who suffer from chronic depression, and the ailments that often accompany it, regard every new development with guarded hope. Many of them have spent their lives trying the latest remedy or enduring treatments that alleviate their symptoms temporarily only to leave them plummeting toward depression again. Until she began to use HeartMath techniques, Sherrie had had a similar experience.

I was born depressed. Literally. Even my baby pictures look sad. Depression runs in my family. One of my uncles received multiple electroshock treatments but ultimately committed suicide anyway. I used to think I was cursed by my own DNA. With my genetics and conditioning—and the absence of any tools to work with life's obstacles—it did not take long for my fragile physiology to give way.

By the time I was seven, my parents had sent me to play cards with a bearded Santa psychiatrist. Thus began my pattern of viewing feelings and emotions as an illness.

When I hit puberty, my "sick" emotions made me physically sick and expressed themselves as severe hormone imbalances, irritable bowel syndrome, PMS, anorexia, and other physical problems. Over the years I bounced from doctor to psychiatrist to psychologist to meditation to yoga to extreme diets of beans and bitter vegetables to acupuncture to [craniosacral] massage to trips in nature to this religion or spiritual practice and that medical procedure to this to that and to the other. You name it and I tried it. Some things worked for a short time, but then the inevitable return of despair would slam me back into a state of powerless resignation.

Before I had the HeartMath tools, I was at a loss to meet life's challenges. I made life's challenges signify that I was imperfect or biologically impaired and unequipped—or that the world was a hostile and unjust place. With HeartMath tools, life's challenges have taken on a completely different meaning and shape for me. They have truly become stepping-stones to greater and greater fulfillment and joy.

Now I can see emotions, in themselves, are not illness. Anyone can be knocked down by difficult events if they do not have the tools to deal with them. Without the tools, we get depressed. With the tools, those same life events can catapult us to new horizons of understanding and empowerment.

An Increasing Rate of Depression

The World Health Organization predicts that by 2020, depression will surpass heart disease as the number one disability worldwide (Murray and Lopez 1996). Older people tend to have higher rates of depression and the U.S. Census Bureau projects that by 2020, nearly one-third of the U.S. population will be over the age of fifty. Even now, experts estimate that nearly one in six Americans over age sixty-five suffers from serious, persistent symptoms of depression (Brody 1998).

The rate of depression for adults and children alike is expected to continue to grow at an alarming rate (Murray and Lopez 1996). It's not hard to understand why. Our world today provokes tremendous anxiety and uncertainty about so many things: family stability, relationship security, job security, health and health care costs, the price of oil and gas, personal and national debt, fear of bird flu or other pandemics, terrorism and wars, the political situation, the growing number of natural disasters, pollution, global warming, species extinction, and even the survival of the planet. Anxiety and uncertainty can result in loss of hope.

Then there's the speedup of communication about all of these things, which requires faster emotional processing than has ever been demanded of people before. When people can't make sense of what's going on and have no previous context for it, you can see how the accumulation of uncertainty and anxiety could put their emotional systems on full-tilt alert.

Overload, frustration, and anxiety create a *static buildup* in the emotional system that eventually results in low-grade depression.

The questions everyone needs to pause and ask themselves are these: How long can people keep up with this accelerating rate of uncertainty? What will be the ongoing emotional and health consequences? What can people do to shore up their emotional systems to sustain hope and prevent depression? In order to live, not just survive, in the twenty-first century, people need to raise their thresholds of emotional overreaction—and they can, once they know how.

Emotional Sensitivity

Feelings are very sensitive by nature. They touch the essence of who you are. So when you feel judged or blamed for having certain feelings, you may learn to repress them. But as we have said, repressed emotions don't just go away. It's an illusion to think that your attempt to rationally control your feelings will eliminate their influence. Even when feelings are vented, it's only a temporary release. Feelings don't go away until they're resolved. Unresolved feelings fester in the unconscious and skew your perceptions of yourself and how you relate to others and to life.

Some people are oversensitive and don't know how to manage their emotional reactions. They easily fall prey to "overcaring," overattachment, and anxious, sad, and depressed states. Emotional sensitivity has been viewed by society as a weakness, especially in men. Perhaps this is why when men feel depressed, they tend to bury their feelings in overwork or mask them through use of stimulants, like alcohol, drugs, and so forth. Depression in men typically shows up as irritability, anger, and discouragement. Women may also use stimulants to mask feelings. Their depression often shows up as a state of hopelessness and helplessness. The fact is, male or female, everyone has emotional sensitivities. The real weakness is when feelings get buried yet control how you perceive and act while you deny that they are having any influence over your perceptions or stability.

Today the survival of the world can be threatened by a lack of emotional stability of a few people. No magic pill will fix that. Unresolved feelings often end up in heartache and heartbreak, causing a feeling of hollowness, like a hole in the heart. People can learn from heartache, but just as often, they end up trapped in hurt, blame, resignation, and loss of hope. The anguish leads to a lot of misunderstandings, even hatred and revenge. The result is what you see every day on the news: one person or group trying to wrest control from another person or group in order to enforce their position, without understanding the feeling worlds or the emotional consequences.

The planet clearly needs more people who can become emotionally aware, responsible citizens. Yet emotional responsibility can seem unappealing to those who want to be free to do as they wish, regardless of whom it affects—including themselves. Others have tried to manage their frustration, anxiety, or depression but haven't been successful and have given up. The real breakthrough and hope is that people *can* manage and transform these emotions.

Emotional Responsibility

The almost instant TV and Web coverage of devastating crimes, natural disasters, and terrorist attacks has an unexpected and important upside. People are now connected to what others throughout the world are thinking and feeling as never before. On-the-scene interviews and vivid, real-time images are making people throughout the world more conscious of the fact that all human beings have similar feelings, hopes, and fears. This new connectivity is creating a *planetary shift* in how people view themselves and each other. It's challenging their opinions, belief systems, and self-centeredness. No one knows exactly where global connectivity is leading to, but everyone knows the stakes are high.

While you can't control the planetary shift, you can control your emotional responses to what's occurring. When you're depressed, you feel lonely and disconnected, so you may think you're not part of all this connectivity. But you *are*, because millions of people feel the same way you do. When you're depressed, you often feel helpless and unable to take on emotional responsibility, but you *can*, in steps, and that is what this book is about. Each step taken brings in a glimmer of light and hope that empowers you to take the next step and the next.

Emotional responsibility is an empowerment process that has "make sense" and "can do," that is, you gain insights that make sense to you and you gain the power to act on them. Empowerment provides meaningfulness and purposeful intent to your efforts to uncover the root causes of your depression and to transform your emotional state into new peace and satisfaction. Transformation allows you to take back emotional control of your life.

Certain emotional needs are universal—to care and be cared for, to have hope, and to feel secure. Answering these needs requires more than physical health, the pursuit of wealth, or a successful career. Answering these needs requires a power beyond intellect. The answer lies in the power of the human heart.

The Heart—A Transformation Agent

It's no coincidence that ancient cultures from Greece to China looked at the heart as a primary source of feeling, virtue, and intelligence. They felt that only through the heart could greed be replaced by charity, selfishness by compassion, and fear by love. Religions all over the world talk about the heart as the seat of the soul and the doorway to spirit or higher self. The ancient Chinese considered the heart as the primary organ capable of influencing and directing people's emotions, morality, decision-making ability, and attainment of inner balance. The ancient Chinese characters for "anguish," "thinking," "thought," "intent," "listen," "virtue," as well as "compassion" and "love" each include a glyph for "heart."

Western languages also refer to the heart both as a physical organ and as a metaphor for feeling, intuition, and the center of people's personalities or beings. After all, it's in the area of the heart that people experience the feeling of many emotions like joy, love, hurt, and sadness. All languages are filled with meaningful phrases like "losing heart," "having heart," "being heartfelt," "playing with a lot of heart," "going deep in your heart to find an answer," and so forth.

It was only in the 1990s that scientists discovered that, in fact, there *is* a link between the physical and the feeling heart—and therein resides the missing link to emotional transformation. It is important to understand this scientific discovery, which we will describe in chapter 4, since it helped shape the HeartMath system—the tools and techniques you will learn to unleash the transforming power and intelligence of your own heart.

You will regain your emotional senses—your sense of hope, sense of belonging, sense of security, and sense of purpose. You will gain your own insights that confirm what you really know inside and that just feel right. There is intelligence in the heart that is designed to help people adjust to the speedup of change so that you have more clarity as you go through life and more power to clear feelings quickly. You will learn how to use the speedup of the planetary shift to your advantage for rapid, manageable, positive change.

✐ How the Planetary Shift Is Affecting You

Write your answers to the following items in the journal or notebook we suggest you keep while you read this book. At the end of the book, you will be asked to review these questions again.

1. List the treatments or approaches (for example, drugs, herbal treatments, talk therapies, self-help methods, nutrition programs, or exercise programs) you have been using to help lift your depression or improve your moods. Next to each one, write what effect it has had, helpful or not helpful. If you stopped the treatment, explain why.

2. List the things in your life or life in general that have caused you to feel the most uncertain, insecure, or stressed over the past few years.

3. Which of these uncertainties contributed to your discouragement or loss of hope?

4. List the things in your life now that cause you to feel the most overloaded, frustrated, or anxious.

5. On a scale of 1 (very low) to 5 (very high), estimate your threshold of emotional reactivity—that is, how quickly you become triggered and get irritated, impatient, frustrated, or anxious.

chapter 3

Clearing Emotions as You Go

Almost everyone feels and talks about the speedup of change that we referred to in chapter 2 as a planetary shift. The accelerating pace of the speedup produces a *shift energy,* which sometimes can feel like riding a wave but at other times feels like being tossed around or caught in an undertow.

These are not just surfing metaphors. We are talking about real electromagnetic waves that are generated by another person's emotional state or by a collective emotional state. That's why you can feel uplifted by the energy in a room of people listening to a dynamic, positive speaker, or sad and depressed at a funeral of someone you didn't even know. People's emotional waves affect themselves and others. We call this *emotional energetics.*

People need to take emotional responsibility to keep pace with a shift energy that keeps speeding up and not let the changing, often chaotic emotional energetics keep getting to them. Negative emotional energies can spread like a virus. Here's an example of how it works. You hear people standing by the copier at work, stressed and complaining, and it causes you to feel more tension and stress. You take out your stress by being impatient with a customer who calls asking for help. The customer gets angry and takes out her stress by yelling at her kids.

Because the shift energy is not going to stop, and the emotional virus is going to continue to spread, people need to learn emotional energy maintenance to clear up their stress as they go. We can't put enough emphasis on this.

You *can* clear as you go in order to be in phase with the shift so your energies and feelings don't spread or back up in your system—then down the tubes you go mentally and emotionally!

Start with Now

It's important to start *now* in transforming depression—whether you are recovering from or hoping to prevent depressive episodes. Many psychological therapies for depression begin by trying to identify stressful events that happened in the past and may have laid the groundwork for depression. We take a different approach. We suggest you start by learning to clear current feelings as you go so you don't pile more on top of any unresolved emotions stored in your cells.

Once your emotions get disturbed, they can quickly draw you back into old emotional habit patterns that you have been trying to clear or thought you had already cleared. Using a one-minute tool right at the moment of disturbance will help you learn to deal with feelings as soon as they come up. Otherwise, in the acceleration of the planetary shift, old stored feelings of disappointment and blame get retriggered.

You may not even know why you are feeling disturbed, irritable, sad, or depressed. And if you get pulled back into rehashing those feelings, the negative energy starts to draw the content back into consciousness (who did what, where, and why) from memories of insecurities, stresses, or traumas of the past that are stored in your cells. The negative energy starts stacking up again, and you only feel worse. Resignation and depression set in.

It takes emotional energetic maintenance in the present to start to clear emotional habits and imprinted memories. People have to take on that emotional energy responsibility. Once you understand how it works and use tools to help you take that responsibility, you build power to surf through the electromagnetic waves of uncertainty and change.

Notice and Ease

The first step is to transform your reactions to all the stressors that are coming up due to global changes and ongoing uncertainties and insecurities so that those same reactions don't keep diminishing your quality of life. The first two tools we're going to give you are called "Notice and Ease" and "Power of Neutral."

You use Notice and Ease as soon as you start to feel anxious, tense, worried, or sad. It's important to *notice*—become emotionally aware and acknowledge what you feel—and *ease*—"befriend" the reaction by holding it in your heart, then letting the feeling ease out of your system. If you try to fight your feelings or try to push them away, they will just gain energy. Befriending your feelings with the Notice and Ease tool takes the intensity or steam out and helps you clear the passing energy. Keep using this tool for one minute or longer until you feel something lighten up, even if you don't get to a complete release yet.

So often, in the midst of shift energies, you can feel so many of these feelings—anxiety, tension, worry, and sadness—all within five or ten minutes! Don't let this confuse you. Don't even try to figure out why. Just keep practicing Notice and Ease until your energies come back into balance. Then listen to the intuitive guidance of your heart on what to do next.

✐ Tool: Notice and Ease

Step 1. Notice and admit what you are feeling.

Step 2. Try to name and befriend the feeling.

Step 3. Tell yourself to e-a-s-e—as you gently focus your attention in the area of your heart, relax as you breathe, and e-a-s-e the stress out.

Feelings are like a code that contains information. You have to name and befriend your feelings to decipher the code. Admit the truth of your feeling world and allow new intuitive perceptions to come to you. As soon as you honestly admit and befriend what you are feeling, you will start to diminish its power over you.

Even a little ease can bring some release and a more balanced perspective. Even if you have to use the tool twenty to thirty times a day or more, do it as often as you need to. It will help build your power to clear as you go. Practice Notice and Ease for one minute or longer whenever you experience the following emotions or attitudes:

- anger
- anxiety
- feeling blocked up

- angst
- blame (of people, situations, or life)
- boredom

- depression
- fear
- numbness
- pouting
- resentment

- resistance
- self-blame
- stubbornness
- worry

- edginess
- guilt
- feeling overwhelmed
- pressure
- resignation and hopelessness

- sadness
- strain
- tension

Power of Neutral

The second one-minute tool is the Power of Neutral tool. Once your emotions get disturbed, your mind will tend to jump in with judgments toward yourself or others. The mind is like a computer. It sees a disturbed feeling as a key press to start a process—analyzing why, calculating next steps, and bringing up memories of what happened when you felt like that before. The Power of Neutral tool helps you put this mental momentum on pause so you can neutralize your reactions and thoughts. Power of Neutral stops the energy drain and allows your heart intelligence to come in.

When you keep judging yourself or others, that energy backs up in your system and feels terrible. It doesn't bring helpful solutions. It only makes you feel disappointed in yourself, which drains more energy. You can stop this in its tracks with Power of Neutral. Keep using the Power of Neutral tool throughout the day to prevent or recoup emotional energy loss and the physical drain that comes with it. Again, even if you have to practice becoming neutral twenty to thirty times a day, do so. It will help you increase your empowerment to stop draining judgmental habits.

🖉 *Tool: Power of Neutral*

Step 1. Take a time-out, breathing slowly and deeply. Imagine the air entering and leaving through the heart area or the center of your chest.

Step 2. Try to disengage from your stressful thoughts and worried feelings as you continue to breathe.

Step 3. Continue the process until you have neutralized the emotional charge.

Practicing Power of Neutral helps bring your mind, emotions, and physiology into a state of neutral. Think of *neutral* as a "time-out zone" where you can step back, neutralize your emotions, and see more options with objective clarity.

Use step 1 as soon as you feel your emotions starting to amp up. First, take a time-out, by choosing to step back from your emotions. The heart breathing in step 1 will help you draw the energy out of your head, where negative thoughts and feelings get amplified. Breathe slowly and deeply in a casual way, as you pretend the breath is going in and out through your heart area.

In step 2, disengage from your stressful thoughts and feelings as you continue to breathe. Just having the intent to disengage can help you release a lot of the emotional energy.

In step 3, you continue the process until you have chilled out and neutralized the emotional charge. This doesn't mean that irritability, anxiety, or other stressful feelings will have totally evaporated. It just means that the charged energy has been taken out and you have stopped accumulating stress. Even if you can't totally neutralize a reaction in the moment, just making the effort to shift into neutral will stop the accumulation of anxiety or stress about it. It will give you a chance to regroup your energies and refocus.

One of the things that can help you get to neutral is asking yourself, "Do I really want to keep draining energy and stressing about the situation or about how bad I feel?" For example, right before a situation that normally makes you anxious or stressed, you may start negatively projecting the idea that you will panic or be judged by others. This is the perfect time to use Power of Neutral—otherwise your emotional reaction will take over and drain you. Instead, you can build your power to be neutral about disturbed feelings and thoughts that won't release right away, so they don't take over and wear you out.

An important first step in transforming depression is to clean up anxieties and judgments *when they come up*. As soon as you feel your energy going sideways, you can use Power of Neutral to refocus within yourself and go back to the heart. This will clear your emotions as you go and start to build your empowerment to clear more.

As stress continues to increase, people will recognize that it is up to them to upgrade their own psychology. Fortunately, it's not that hard to do. Notice and Ease and Power of Neutral provide you with emotional survival skills, but more than that, they provide you with emotional rewards of insight and self-respect. Using these two tools requires a genuine, meaningful intent to clear your emotions as you go. As you build your ability to use these tools, you will acquire a new type of emotional energy maintenance that everyone will need to learn in order to keep pace with the speedup of events as the planetary shift continues.

Not Enough Time

When we ask people who attend HeartMath training programs what their biggest stressor is, the majority say, "Not having enough time!" Because they don't have enough time to keep up with everything, they multitask, get distracted, and routinely become impatient, irritable, frustrated, or anxious when things don't go as planned.

What they are really saying is that their emotional system isn't able to keep pace, so their minds are going nuts trying to figure out how to cope! Many admit they are too stressed to do anything about their stress. They don't realize that their emotional energy is backing up in their systems and causing the overload.

Emotion is energy—*feeling in motion*. Perceptions trigger thoughts and attitudes, which trigger feelings, which in turn trigger thoughts and attitudes. It's an ongoing spiral. If you could see it in slow motion, you'd see that you're either spiraling up or spiraling down when you're in this process. You're either renewing energy or draining energy.

The most powerful interception of a downward spiral is taking emotional responsibility. It starts with watching your emotional energetics.

The term "emotional energetics" may sound abstract or esoteric, but it's really not. Everyone has experienced energetics. When you hear someone say, "I can't handle his energy," what she is really saying is, "His emotions are getting to me." How you handle your own emotional energies will determine how you respond to others'. Emotional energy maintenance is what you do to keep yourself from overreacting or getting drained.

Emotional energetics are first expressed inside, in your feelings, thoughts, and attitudes, before they either get expressed externally or get repressed. Emotional energy maintenance is learning to clear emotions to save energy and achieve more effective outcomes.

Make a commitment to stand behind your heart intent to clear as you go. Practice the tools to keep stress from stacking up, draining your energy, then playing out in mental, emotional, and/or physical ailments. A stackup from not clearing is what causes most short- or long-term depression. Look at it as a formula:

Lack of clearing = depression.

Once you learn this formula, you can start to do something about it.

Hinge Points

Practice the Notice and Ease and Power of Neutral tools when your emotions get triggered, and soon you'll begin to notice what we call *hinge points.*

Your emotional habits propel you to judge, blame, vent, or repress feelings, while your heart intuition whispers, "Let it go. It's not a big deal." This is a hinge point—a moment where you choose to go one way or another. This is where you can learn to be heart intelligent and direct your emotional energy so it won't wash back on you with more stress. That's how you take emotional responsibility.

Learn to increase the percentage of times you make a heart choice at the hinge points. In this way, you will build your overall heart intelligence rather than always falling back into the typical old patterns that keep compounding your stress. As your ratio of heart choices increases, your heart-intelligent thoughts will become louder and the old patterns will gradually lose strength.

Because those automatic mental and emotional habit patterns have become etched in your neural circuits over time, they won't disappear overnight. But with just a little practice of unleashing the power of your heart, the old patterns will start to come under management and then they will clear. The stored energy released will transform into new feelings of peace and satisfaction that inspire you to keep practicing.

Here are some things to watch for at hinge points:

1. When, out of habit, confusion, or just plain stubbornness, you make a choice that leads to more stress, drain, and fatigue, remind yourself that you're not "bad." If you feel or think you're bad or get disappointed in yourself, you will only add needless stress on top of stress, which will delay your opportunity to clear. When this happens, use Notice and Ease. Befriend the feelings and keep using the tools. Use the tools as if you were pressing Restart or Refresh on a computer. Treat and clear feelings from now—*a new now*—and stop stacking up stress and energy drains.

2. Remember you are not alone. Millions are going through this same process. They fall back into their same old, stress-creating mental and emotional habits and experience the emotional energy backwash from it on a daily basis. It's standard. Have compassion for yourself. The emotional backwash from stored-up stress can feel like a heaviness or weight in the area of your heart or even like a wave or wall of resistance against your chest. You can let any angst about these feelings go because you are getting educated in what's going on and how to get to a new emotional frontier.

3. Know that it can be hard to let the angst go. The mind will jump in to try to figure ways to get rid of an awful

feeling. The mind goes through the same old merry-go-round that has never resolved anything before. Instead, it just stirs up more angst! A mind-on-mind struggle can't create clearing. So it gets down to the heart. That's why we keep introducing the heart and provide the HeartMath tools. There is intelligence and power in the heart, designed to align the mind with the heart so you can gain more clarity and power to clear your emotions more quickly.

Start practicing Notice and Ease to move through any stress backwash, and then apply Power of Neutral to stop the energy drain and lift you into more objectivity. These two tools will help you create alignment between your heart and mind at the hinge point. This heart alignment will help you make the heart choice that goes against the grain of your automatic reactions but feels better to you in the outcome. You'll learn more tools for specific applications in the coming chapters.

In summary, you can become aware of your hinge points — where the backup or the clearing starts. Once you get the signal "This is a hinge point," you know what to do. Use a tool to go back to your heart and get your heart and mind aligned. Listen to your heart intelligence and follow it. If you don't do what you really know in your heart, it's because there's a stubborn resistance from the old pattern. (That's also standard, and it doesn't make you bad either.) Just recognize and befriend the resistance with compassion.

Very often, in order to be able to clear a stubborn resistance, you have to become heart vulnerable with yourself or with an understanding friend. Becoming vulnerable with yourself means having an honest and sincere talk with your heart, while you're compassionately befriending the stress you feel. That's what people try to do when they take a walk on the beach or in the woods to clear their mind and feelings. Being heart vulnerable while using the Notice and Ease and Power of Neutral tools, you can take that walk on the beach or gain release or insight wherever you are.

Look at the above three points as a formula. By using the formula, you'll catch more hinge points and make heart choices that enable you to surf the waves and not get caught in as many undertows.

There will always be times that you miss a hinge point and the backwash from the emotional energetics gets you. Recognize that's what it is. Tell yourself, "No big deal." Don't add drama to it. Just increase your meaningful intent to make the shift. Don't think you were bad or assign guilt or extra significance to it, as that will only pull you down further into the undertow. Use these tools and the others you will learn in this book with heartfelt, meaningful intent until you're back on your surfboard, and then move on.

Above all, realize *everyone* is having to play this same game. They either clear or stack stress as they go. Look at the speedup of hinge-point options in the shift as a video game that everyone is in. You now have an understanding of how it works, and you have the tools to play the game better. Using the formula, you will not only keep up with the shift, you will ride the waves and accomplish more as you clear more. This will bring new hope that you can turn the shift energies and speed of change to your advantage.

chapter 4

The New Science of Emotional Transformation

There has been promising new research on the power of positive emotions in the past decade. Prior to that, studies on emotions focused almost exclusively on negative emotional states that cause suffering, like fear, anxiety, depression, anger, and hostility. *Positive psychology* is the name of a movement started in the early twenty-first century to focus on positive emotions that make life most worth living (Seligman and Csikszentmihalyi 2000; Snyder and Lopez 2002).

Studies on positive emotions are now enabling researchers to better understand mood disorders and provide new therapies to help people achieve more stable, positive emotional states. Research done at the Institute of HeartMath and other institutions is providing new hope for people with depression, anxiety, and other stress-related disorders. We are bringing to light powerful yet simple techniques that you can use to improve how you feel, think, and perceive life—techniques that increase heart intelligence and mental clarity, that help you regulate your brain chemicals and hormones, that bring you more natural highs. This is the real fountain of youth that people have been searching for over the centuries. With a little education and genuine practice, you can move into a new experience of life so rewarding that you will be motivated to keep regulating your emotions to sustain the good feelings. The payoff is delicious in terms of improved quality of life.

Some of the research at HeartMath emerged from a new field called *neurocardiology* and the study of heart-brain interactions. Scientists in this field have made some astounding discoveries about the heart. Our own research on heart-brain communication is presented in more detail in our other books and on the Institute of HeartMath website (www.heart math.org). In this chapter, we will give you a brief overview of some of this new research on the heart and why it is bringing new hope to people with depression.

Heart-Brain Communication

It was during the 1990s that scientists discovered the heart has its own "little brain" that *functions independently* from the brain in the head. This intrinsic cardiac nervous system or "brain" can sense, feel, learn, and remember (Armour 1991; Armour and Kember 2004). The heart actually sends more information to the brain "upstairs," telling it what to do, than the brain sends to the heart (Cameron 2002). This discovery is revolutionizing scientific thinking that previously viewed heart-brain communication essentially as a one-way conversation—with the brain barking orders that the heart passively obeyed.

Not only does the heart have its own little brain, it produces its own hormones. When this was discovered in the mid-1980s, the heart was reclassified as a hormonal gland (Cantin and Genest 1986). The heart produces large quantities of oxytocin, the love or bonding hormone secreted during mother-child bonding after birth and during satisfying sex, and ANP, a stress-balancing hormone that has receptors in the brain (Cantin and Genest 1986; Gutkowska et al. 2000).

Heart Rate Variability

Also in the early 1990s, our research team at the Institute of HeartMath discovered that the pattern of the heart's rhythmic activity changes as different emotions are experienced (McCraty et al. 1995; Tiller, McCraty, and Atkinson 1996). "Heart rate variability" is a term used to refer to the natural changes in heart rate that occur from one heartbeat to the next. When these increases and decreases in heart rate are plotted over time, they give rise to a *pattern* of heart activity that is called the *heart rhythm*. Signals generated by the heart's rhythmic activity are sent to the brain and throughout the body. Your brain, respiratory, and digestive systems all respond to the heart's rhythm. Each of these systems also generates its own oscillating rhythm. Because the heart's rhythm is the most powerful, it can bring other systems into synchronization with it. This means that your respiratory and digestive systems and your higher brain functions all dance to the beat of the heart's rhythmic pattern.

When you're experiencing positive emotions, like sincere appreciation, care, joy, compassion, or love, your heart's rhythms are harmonious, creating an ordered, coherent pattern that helps bring your whole body into increased harmony and coherence. When you're experiencing negative emotions, like frustration, hurt, anger, anxiety, hopelessness, or depression, your heart's rhythms become disordered and chaotic, and your whole body falls into stress (McCraty et al. 2006).

In addition, the electromagnetic fields generated by the heart's chaotic or coherent rhythms are transmitted like radio waves throughout the body and to other people in close proximity. This helps explain how other people's emotional states can affect you (McCraty 2004; McCraty et al. 2006).

Heart-Brain Coherence

The power to transform emotions involves learning how to bring your heart, brain, and nervous system into *synchronization* or *coherence*. Researchers have found that when people learn how to intentionally shift the pattern of their heart's rhythm into a more coherent or synchronized mode, their emotional state improves quickly (McCraty et al. 2006; McCraty and Tomasino 2006). You can shift into heart rhythm coherence while you are relaxed or energized, whether your heart rate is 50 or 130 beats per minute. Heart rhythm coherence has important implications for peak performance.

In figure 4.1, the top graph shows a woman's disordered heart rhythm pattern while she was feeling frustrated and anxious and the bottom graph shows the coherent heart rhythm pattern of the same person after she used a HeartMath tool and was feeling appreciation. You can see that her heart rate stayed the same, varying between about 60 and 90 beats per minute, whether her heart rhythm pattern was incoherent or coherent.

Heart rhythm coherence renews and revitalizes. It enhances your heart's connection with your core spirit and with other people. It downloads more spirit or higher consciousness into your human system and builds resilience to navigate an increasingly complex and uncertain world. It also helps bring you emotional textures that are more uplifting and fulfilling.

Coherence is an even more powerful physiological state than relaxation. It is considered an optimal state for healing, learning, emotional transformation, and peak performance (McCraty et al. 2006).

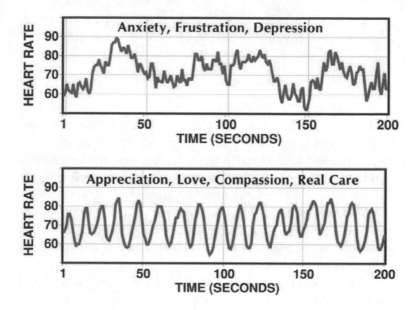

Figure 4.1

The top graph shows the irregular, jagged heart rhythm pattern typical of stressful feelings like anger, frustration, worry, and anxiety. This is called an *incoherent* pattern. The bottom graph shows the heart rate variability or heart rhythm pattern typical of appreciation and other positive feelings. This smooth heart rhythm is what scientists call a *highly ordered* or *coherent* pattern and is a sign of good health and emotional balance. ' Institute of HeartMath

In figure 4.2 (on page 48), the top graph shows a typical heart rhythm pattern for the emotion of anger on the left and the power spectrum of this heart rhythm on the right. The power spectrum for anger shows the activity of the sympathetic nervous system (high peak at the left), the parasympathetic nervous system (tiny peak at the right), and the activity in the heart-brain communication loop (tiny peak in the middle).

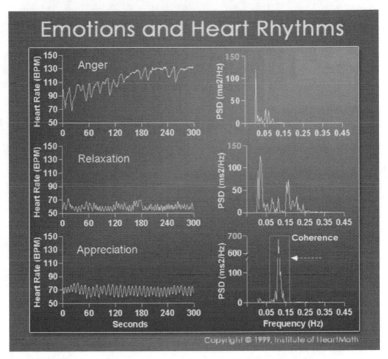

Figure 4.2
The graphs to the left show typical heart rhythm patterns during states of anger, relaxation, and appreciation. The graphs to the right show the corresponding power spectra of the heart rhythm patterns at left. The power spectra provide a window into the activity of the two branches of the autonomic nervous system and activity in the heart-brain communication loop during each state (see detailed description in text). ' Institute of HeartMath

The middle graph shows a typical heart rhythm pattern and power spectrum for relaxation. This power spectrum shows more parasympathetic activity. Relaxation will increase parasympathetic activity and lower heart rate, but it won't create synchronization or coherence.

The bottom graph shows a typical heart rhythm pattern for appreciation (which is similar to that produced by many sincere positive emotions). In this power spectrum there is one large, narrow peak, which indicates increased synchronization and harmony between the sympathetic and parasympathetic nervous systems and in the communication between the heart and brain. Look at the topmost number on the vertical scale in each power spectrum graph, which indicates the amount of power. In the spectra for both anger and relaxation, the largest peak measures under 150. In contrast, the peak for appreciation (coherence) measures 700! *Synchronization and coherence generate more than five times the power!* This is the empowerment that you need to help lift depression.

Your sympathetic nervous system gets activated when you are under stress to prepare your body to react to threats, real or imagined, while your parasympathetic nervous system calms things down. Chronic stress, anxiety, depression, and social isolation are associated with an overactive sympathetic nervous system. The chronic activation of the sympathetic nervous system due to negative emotional states increases the risk of stress-related disorders, heart rhythm disturbances, heart attacks, and sudden cardiac death (Rozanski, Blumenthal, and Kaplan 1999; Arnetz and Ekman 2006; Molinare, Compare, and Parati 2006).

As you learn how to shift into heart rhythm coherence, you increase your power to change your mood more quickly and *set a new pattern* of emotional state and healthier functioning (McCraty and Tomasino 2006). The HeartMath tools and techniques have been scientifically designed and validated to help you empower and transform negative emotional states like anger, stress, anxiety, and depression.

Stress and the Brain

The part of the brain that gets activated under stress stays active long after stressful situations are over, which may explain why it's hard for many people to let stressful feelings go. And the brain is also a pattern-matching system that scans for what's familiar. When a stressful situation occurs, the brain scans its memory banks looking for previous stressful experiences until it perceives a match. Then it triggers the same emotional reactions you had the previous time—like anxiety, hurt, resignation, or depression. The same neurotransmitters and biochemicals are then released into your system. If your body experiences a particular emotional state repeatedly, the neural circuits for that state are reinforced, which means you've literally built in a physical pathway that makes it easier to feel those stressful emotions.

The neural connections going from the emotional centers in the brain to the cognitive or thinking centers are actually stronger and more plentiful than the wiring going in the other direction (LeDoux 1996). That's why it's hard to have rational control over your emotions. The good news is that all these brain circuits are flexible and can be reshaped with new patterns throughout life. It's never too late to learn or to change. Since emotional processes work faster than thinking, it takes a power stronger than just mental processes to repattern negative emotional circuitry. It takes the power of the coherent heart.

Scientists have discovered that the heart's signals have a significant effect on the brain's cognitive and emotional functions, continuously influencing how people perceive and respond to the world as well as how they feel (Pribram and Melges 1969; McCraty et al. 2006; McCraty and Tomasino 2006). Heart rhythm coherence helps synchronize cortical activity, facilitating higher cognitive faculties, such as perception, memory, discernment, and problem solving. A coherent heart rhythm also communicates a message of well-being to the brain's emotional circuitry. As your heart rhythm changes, so does the electrical activity in the cells of the amygdala, the key emotional memory center in the brain. In fact, the cells in the amygdala have been shown to be synchronized to the heart-beat (Frysinger and Harper 1990). Through these and other pathways, familiar emotional patterns like fear or depression can be repatterned by harnessing the power of your heart.

You can learn how to work with the magnificent system of your heart and brain to change your neural circuitry and trigger different neurotransmitters and biochemistry. You can keep your emotional maintenance on par.

Cortisol and Depression

Cortisol has been called "the mother" of all stress hormones. Your adrenal glands produce large amounts of cortisol when you are under stress. Cortisol increases blood sugar levels to help you better cope with the stress. Ongoing emotional stress can reset your body's cortisol production to increased levels so that even when you try to relax, you still feel stressed. Many people with depression maintain high levels of cortisol in their body, due to ongoing stress. High cortisol levels may also contribute to depression.

Heart Rate Variability and Depression

Stress is reflected in disordered and chaotic heart rhythm patterns. Over time, this causes wear and tear on the nervous system and can lead to a lowering of heart rate variability

(HRV). This means that your heart rate isn't as adaptable as it should be. It doesn't increase fast enough when you sit up quickly or climb stairs, so you feel faint or winded. It doesn't slow down fast enough either, making it difficult to relax or sleep. This lack of flexibility is a predictor of many diseases, any one of which can kill you (Tsuji et al. 1994; Dekker et al. 1997). To make matters worse, low HRV may indicate lower emotional flexibility as well, so when things do go badly, you find it harder to cope.

On the other hand, increased HRV shows a positive correlation to improved mood. Several studies have found links between HRV and treatments for major depression. One study found that patients who felt better after taking antidepressants showed an increase in HRV (Balogh et al. 1993). Another study found that when cognitive behavioral therapy was given to depressed heart patients and their depression lifted, HRV improved at the same time (Carney et al. 2000).

When Therapy Works

Simply put, when therapies work, people feel better. Their mood and outlook improve. They experience more optimistic attitudes and positive feelings. We believe that cognitive therapies or emotional healing methods work best when they introduce coherent rhythmic patterns from the heart to help people neutralize negative emotional energy and shift into positive emotional states.

Researchers are still trying to understand exactly how positive attitudes and emotions affect human brain functions and neurochemicals. According to positive psychology research, when you're experiencing a negative emotion, the range of thoughts available to your mind is limited, resulting in fixated and more predictable thinking and action. Positive emotions produce patterns of thought that are more flexible and inclusive, and they lead to more creative action (Isen 1999; Fredrickson 2002).

Positive emotions also have an "undoing effect" on negative emotions. They loosen the hold that negative emotions have on your brain and body. Positive emotions seem to serve as effective antidotes for the lingering effects of negative emotions (Fredrickson 2002).

One purpose of HeartMath tools is to help you cultivate more positive emotions. The tools teach you how to shift out of a negative emotional state into a positive one (psychologically and physiologically)—right in the midst of stress—in order to gain a more heart-intelligent perspective.

University of Michigan positive psychology researcher Barbara Fredrickson says, "positive emotions can have effects beyond making people 'feel good' or improving their subjective experiences of life. They also have the potential to broaden people's habitual modes of thinking and build their physical, intellectual, and social resources" (2000, 4). Furthermore, Fredrickson notes, these resources last longer than the transient positive emotional states that led to their acquisition and can be drawn upon in future moments, when people are in different emotional states, to help them overcome current stresses faster and to make them more resilient to future adversities. Thus, "through experiences of positive emotions, people transform themselves, becoming more creative, knowledgeable, resilient, socially integrated, and healthy individuals" (2002, 123). Based on her work, Fredrickson also suggests that "intervention strategies that cultivate positive emotions are particularly suited for preventing and treating problems rooted in negative emotions, such as anxiety, depression, aggression, and stress-related health problems" (2002, 1).

Cognitive Behavioral Therapy

Cognitive behavioral therapy (CBT) is the most common form of psychotherapeutic treatment for depression. CBT helps you analyze your way out of negative thoughts and emotions. Cognitive therapy asks you to challenge negative assumptions and the content of your thoughts and to take a more rational approach toward your emotions. CBT works with the mind. But mind-on-mind efforts don't always shift your emotional state. Your mind can be telling you to shift, while your emotions keep heaving. It's hard to get a grip on stubborn emotions. It takes coherent heart power and heart intention to effectively rearrange your emotions so they don't keep rearranging you.

People have some heart intention in whatever they do to help themselves—but if the emotional patterns are strong enough, they can easily override the best intentions. Intentionally activating heart coherence is an accelerated way to free yourself and set a new pattern.

Acceptance and Commitment Therapy

A new therapy that is gaining a lot of attention is called acceptance and commitment therapy (ACT). It was developed by Steven Hayes, past president of the Association for Behavioral and Cognitive Therapies. ACT advises people not to fight negative feelings, but to accept them. ACT then teaches a form of mindfulness, a Buddhist approach to observing thoughts and feelings without identifying with them. After you accept a negative feeling, you use your mind to "disidentify" with it and refocus your attention on your values. ACT helps you make a commitment to connecting with your values and living your values.

Heart Psychology

From our understanding of psychophysiology at HeartMath, it appears that ACT is engaging the heart in the therapeutic process. Acceptance is a heart quality. Acceptance doesn't mean resignation or caving in to negative emotions. It means that you become more neutral toward them so they stop controlling your life.

Negative emotions have their place. Negative emotions aren't bad. They contain information to help you decipher what's going on underneath, what's the truth in your feeling world. When you judge your thoughts or feelings, you add negative energy that increases the density of the feelings and blocks any insights you might gain.

While ACT talks about *accepting*, HeartMath tools refer to it as *befriending*, which means bringing disturbed or negative thoughts and feelings into your heart. Befriending brings compassion to the situation and disarms those feelings so they loosen their hold. Befriending helps the power and intelligence of your heart clear a lot of emotional reactions that keep being triggered.

Acceptance and befriending are attitudes that increase heart rhythm coherence. We call feelings of love, care, compassion, appreciation, and forgiveness *core heart feelings* because they come from the core values of the heart. They are uplifting and feel good to your entire system. When you intentionally generate core heart feelings, you nourish yourself at every level—mental, emotional, physical, and spiritual.

Core heart feelings evoke attitudes such as nonjudgment, appreciation, patience, and respect that come from deep within the heart. The more you commit to intentionally generating these core heart feelings and attitudes toward yourself and others, the more you will align your heart, mind, emotions, and actions so you can live your core values.

It's essential that you know what your deeper values are. Knowing and living your core values brings you self-respect and increases the textures of your life. These values come from your heart. They are part of your heart's intelligence, which intuitively knows what's best for the wholeness of a situation and for the well-being of your system.

HeartMath tools can facilitate CBT, ACT, and other forms of therapy to add more heart psychology to the process. Heart psychology provides a new way to go deeper into the heart, draws on a different source of power to facilitate change, and connects you with your core spirit. It's not a quick fix, but committing to it powers you up so you can do things you haven't been able to do before.

Toni first started to experience feelings of depression when she was a young girl. She remembers feeling sad all the time, just wanting to stay in her room and not play with other children. As she entered her teen years, it got worse. Daily bouts of crying were normal for her. On the outside, she appeared to be on top of the world. She was a good student, well-liked, and a leader. Toni says that putting herself in leadership roles and participating in school activities like cheerleading was just a diversion, an attempt to compensate for the pain and emptiness she felt on the inside.

Her depression continued on into her thirties as she struggled to raise her family and manage her successful career as a professional fundraiser. Toni knew she had a serious problem, and she desperately wanted help. She tried everything from religion and prayer to meditation, therapy, and antidepressants to control her depression but found only random, temporary relief. After years of trying to rid herself of this emotional disease, she finally came to the stark conclusion that she would simply never feel better. All she could experience were feelings of hopelessness.

One day a friend told her about HeartMath. She was tired of chasing a cure for her problem but finally decided to attend a HeartMath program. Toni describes her experience:

During the weekend I made a sincere effort to make contact with my heart, and during an exercise something remarkable happened. I had a breakthrough, a profound experience of hope and release. For days after the seminar I knew something was different, but how could this be? I had had temporary breakthroughs before but always returned to feeling depressed. I feared I would go back into the depths of chronic depression, and after so many years it was hard to accept that by going to my heart I could be free of it.

Toni kept practicing what she had learned, using one of the tools when she felt the need, consciously activating core heart feelings. Within a month the fear of her depression coming back was gone. She knew those old emotional problems were behind her. They seemed like they'd been a bad dream. Her health improved dramatically. A joyfulness, a lightness, and an excitement for life had now replaced her depression. That was ten years ago.

Toni says her life continues to become more fulfilling and enriched, even amidst stressors and challenges, because the tools keep unfolding new awareness and enjoyable emotional textures. Her rather dramatic experience provides a wonderful example of what can happen when your heart comes alive. Emotional problems can be some of the most difficult to deal with, especially if they are long-standing like Toni's. Perhaps she'd looked to her heart for help before, but not knowing what it was supposed to do or exactly how to activate the heart's intelligence with consistency, she continued to suffer for years. Once she did make that deeper heart connection, her emotions responded accordingly and Toni's life took a major turn for the better.

Connecting with Your Spirit

We know from experience that our hearts are our principal point of connection with spirit. Not only does our own subjective experience confirm this, but there is biological evidence to support this as well.

In the fetus, the heart is the first organ to develop, even before the brain stem. Amazingly enough, the heart starts beating on its own without any known physical stimulus. We anticipate that future scientific research will eventually demonstrate that the physical heart is the central distribution station for one's true spirit and intuitive regulation of the mental, emotional, and physical systems.

Fortunately, people do not have to wait for science to develop the measuring instruments to prove the existence of spirit before they connect with the organizing intelligence of their hearts.

The more you experience the state of heart rhythm coherence, the more easily your brain's neural networks can be retrained to a healthier level of functioning. Using HeartMath tools is not simply a psychological process, but over time creates a physiological shift that brings your entire system—heart, brain, mind, emotions, and nervous system—into a dynamic state of coherence. It is in this coherent state that more empowerment and heart intelligence become available for emotional transformation.

Heart intelligence enables you to *adapt* to life's challenges and save emotional energy to regain control of your life. The result is that your life is enriched with value and meaning. Hope appears on the horizon again. As your depression lifts, you unfold potential hidden within your heart that you never knew was there. You become more of who you really are. You become your own hope generator.

chapter 5

Understanding Stress-Induced Depression

Core heart feelings, like love, care, appreciation, compassion, and forgiveness, are what give you the coherent power to *live* your core values. But all too often, a genuine feeling of love or care gets compromised.

Add a little insecurity to your feeling of love for your girlfriend and your mind takes you right into clingy attachment, jealousy, or even paralyzing fear. Get too identified with anything you care about—a job, a child, or an issue—and if things don't go your way, you can feel drained from worry and anxiety. To make things worse, overidentity can leave you feeling like a victim.

Love and care compromised by insecurity, overattachment, or overidentity turn into *lower heart feelings*. You are still caring—about your mate, your child, or your job—so you do still feel some heart. But you are also pulled by overcare or overattachment. These lower heart feelings send fight-or-flight stress signals throughout your body. Insecurity draws energy down from your heart into your solar plexus (located about four inches below the heart, just below the sternum), propelling you to glom on to what you are attached to or to close off your heart in self-protection. Love can turn into jealousy or even hate. Care can turn into anxiety. Appreciation can go out the window and turn into blame. Yet you still can feel some of your original love or care or appreciation.

When you enter this state of mixed heart feelings, your sense of who you really are gets compromised. Someone or something is to blame, but it's your heart that has to pay. After all, it can seem like your heart led you down that road to stress and pain.

Understanding the distinction between uplifting core heart feelings of love or care and distressing lower heart feelings (caused by overcare, overidentity, or overattachment) can clear up a lot of confusion about the language of the heart. It also may help explain why depression and heart disease are so often linked.

Core heart feelings, like care and appreciation, generate coherent heart rhythm patterns. Lower heart feelings, like worry and anxiety, generate incoherent heart rhythms. Learning the distinction within yourself and learning tools to shift from incoherent to coherent heart rhythms is a key to transforming depression and improving heart health. That may seem hard to do when you're feeling stressed or depressed, but there are simple coherence-building tools and techniques to help you make that important shift.

The Quick Coherence Technique

Quick Coherence is a simple yet powerful technique to release distress and bring more coherence into your heart rhythms. Once you've learned the technique, it only takes a minute to do. There are three steps:

Step 1. Heart Focus. Focus your attention in the area of your heart. If this sounds confusing, try this: Focus on your right big toe and wiggle it. Now focus on your right elbow. Now gently focus in the center of your chest, the area of your heart. (Most people think the heart is on the left side of the chest, but it's really closer to the center, behind the breastbone.) You may want to put your hand over your heart to help you keep your focus there. If your mind wanders, just keep shifting your attention back to the area of your heart while you do steps 2 and 3.

Step 2. Heart Breathing. As you focus on the area of your heart, imagine your breath is flowing in and out through that area. This helps your mind and energy to stay focused in the heart area and your respiration and heart rhythms to synchronize. Breathe slowly and gently in through your heart (to a count of five or six) and slowly and easily out through your heart (to a count of five or six). Do this until your breathing feels smooth and balanced, not forced. You may discover that it's easier to find a slow, easy rhythm by counting "one thousand, two thousand," rather than "one, two." Continue to breathe with ease until you find a natural inner rhythm that feels good to you.

Step 3. Heart Feeling. Continue to breathe through the area of your heart. As you do so, recall a positive feeling, a time when you felt good inside, and try to reexperience it. This could be a feeling of appreciation or care toward a special person or a pet, a place you enjoyed, or an activity that was fun. Allow yourself to feel this good feeling of appreciation or care. If you can't feel anything, it's okay; just try to find the attitude of appreciation or care. Once you've found it, try to sustain the attitude by continuing your Heart Focus, Heart Breathing, and Heart Feeling.

Heart Feeling helps you increase coherence without having to remain focused on your breathing rhythm. If it was hard for you to find a positive feeling or attitude, take a moment now to remember a couple of times when you felt uplifting feelings, even if they occurred a long time ago. Write those experiences down or memorize them so they will be easy to recall when you practice Quick Coherence.

Don't worry if you also feel some uncomfortable feelings while you're breathing a positive feeling and attitude. Even a little heart feeling starts to clear blocked emotional energies. Building coherence is a process. Just keep up a genuine heart intention to hold the attitude of love, care, appreciation, compassion, or forgiveness while you practice the Quick Coherence technique.

It's important to practice this one-minute coherence-building technique as soon as you feel overwhelmed, sad, or stressed. You can also practice it after you use Notice and Ease and Power of Neutral. With a sincere use of these two tools and the Quick Coherence technique, you *can* bring overcare, overattachment, and overidentity back to a more balanced and coherent care.

Create a simple and easy practice routine to build coherence, and do it earnestly and genuinely. Start by practicing Quick Coherence first thing in the morning to set up your day. Then use it whenever you feel overwhelmed, sad, or stressed during the day and at night, as the last thing before sleep.

Watch yourself over the next few days and make notes about what commonly triggers overwhelming or depressing attitudes and feelings in you. Observe the rhythm and pattern of those triggers and moods. Use the tools to help prevent and recover from those recurring patterns. You will start to reset your system into increasing coherence.

Developing Intuitive Discernment

Increasing coherence has many mental, emotional, and physical benefits. One of the most important benefits of increased coherence is that it helps you develop *intuitive self-guidance*. Most people think of intuition as psychic ability or as a new invention, like the lightbulb. But a more practical baseline application is developing intuitive discernment of how to move more effectively through day-to-day life. The first and most important way to develop that intuitive discernment is to know when you are in or out of your heart. The more you are in your heart, the more coherence and alignment there is between mind, emotions, and body. It is this *coherent alignment* that allows intuition to flow into the human system.

Intuition is a flow of information from your real spirit. Research at the Institute of HeartMath has shown that intuitive information is registered first in the heart and then transmitted to the brain/mind (McCraty et al. 2004a, 2004b). That's why we call it *heart intuition* or *heart intelligence*.

Quick Coherence practice is like exercising to help develop your intuitive self-guidance system. As you use Quick Coherence and the other coherence-building techniques that you will learn in the next few chapters, you will create the coherent alignment that invites or draws in more of your higher discernment faculties—your intuition—to facilitate clearing stress as you go. You will create a cushion between you and stressors that come up so they don't drain you as much, and you'll have clearer intuition on how to respond. As you build coherent alignment, your intuition will facilitate clearing the stored stress and depression patterns in your cells.

Remember, coherence-building techniques involve putting out a core Heart Feeling or attitude like love, care, appreciation, or nonjudgment, not just Heart Breathing. It's your core heart values and feelings that create intuitive unfoldment and build empowerment to lift depression.

You Can Embrace Change

A lot of people are afraid of change, even if it's positive. They are afraid of letting go of old familiar moods. The familiar, even if it's miserable, is more comfortable. The heart can ease the process of letting go of moods and habits that don't serve you. Learning emotional regulation with Quick Coherence and the other tools will help you take back control of your life so that you can move through change at more of a pace you can handle. Thousands of HeartMath clients have experienced rapid, manageable, positive change through practicing these HeartMath techniques. The practice gives them inner confirmation that they are on the right track.

J. K.'s poignant story illustrates this. J. K., a lawyer who was deployed to the Iraq war, used the Quick Coherence technique to lift his deep depression and help him cope with the stresses of battle and of returning home:

> After I was notified that I was being deployed to Iraq, I was distraught. I went into a deep depression, a dark hole that I saw no way out of. The things I used to enjoy were meaningless to me. I could no longer enjoy my family or friends or girlfriend. I would just sit there counting the minutes until I was to be taken away from them. In boot camp, the depression really took over. I had been a Boston Red Sox fan my whole life, but I felt so depressed at Fort Drum that I slept right through their World Series win. That was when my aunt turned me on to my HeartMath coach.

I was so lucky to be exposed to these tools, right at the most stressful time of my life. Right away, the tools gave me a game plan and a strategy to deal with stress.

My biggest fear before leaving was that I would lose it while I was away. We all saw guys who came back blotto from the emotional stress. The military was preparing us, training us to deal with driving in a convoy and giving us strategies for dealing with an ambush or a chemical attack, but they were not giving us resources or strategies to deal with the ambush of our emotional stress and the attack of our worry. That's what HeartMath gave me, and it was the most important preparation of all.

From the very beginning, my HeartMath coach showed me that I did not have to be a victim of the stress around me and that my emotions and "freak out" were not the enemy. Over and over again before I left, I used the Quick Coherence technique, focusing my attention on the area around my heart and breathing in the feel-great feeling I get when I am skiing—the feeling of the cold and windy air on my face, the freedom of flying down the hill. That would help me calm down and see more clearly how to respond to the situations I was facing. Knowing that I had control over whether I would "lose it" or not lifted my depression, and gave me a sense of power in a situation that I never expected to be in.

I was terrified as we boarded the flight in the middle of the night to take the plane to Iraq. When we arrived, after having been up all night, I was taken in a helicopter to the base where I was to be interviewed by high-ranking officers to see if I was of a caliber to work with them or be sent out into the front lines. A lot was at stake. I was exhausted, scared, unshaven, overwhelmed. I dropped into my heart and started skiing down the slope of the "audition" for superior officers when a mortar attack hit!

My first day and already they were that close—trying to kill us! Talk about a stressful job interview! I did Quick Coherence and handled the situation with calm and poise. Ultimately, I got the position I wanted, working with high-ranking officers and helicopter pilots.

After my ten-month tour of duty, coming home had its own stressors. The heart tools helped me readjust to life in the States and the culture shock it brought. Everyone wanted me to make special time for them. It was stressful to make sure everyone could feel my love for them. At the same time, I needed to readjust to being back. HeartMath helped me communicate my care to them, without overcaring, without getting overwhelmed by their demands, and without saying things ... that I would regret later.

Having practiced HeartMath on a real battlefield, I now use it in the courtroom all the time. HeartMath helps me focus on what I really need to focus on, bringing perspective to my life. It also empowers me to take the significance out of what doesn't matter.

Taking the Significance Out

People assign meaning and significance to what might happen, creating worries and fears that can lead them right into depression. People also assign significance based on previous emotional experiences. They build their reality based on emotional experiences from their past, which influences their current perceptions, reactions, and thought processes.

When you assign too much significance or drama to negative emotional experiences, you end up being consumed by them. Brooding is the mind's attempt to resolve emotional pain, but it doesn't work. It only adds more significance to and overidentity with a negative experience.

It's important to understand how your mind assigns significance and then leads you down a pathway to despair. Here are some typical pathways.

Significance can start with sentimental feelings about how things used to be (real or imagined). Then your mind builds an overattachment to those experiences and convinces you that you'll never be happy again without them. Or you might begin by having sympathy for someone else's problem, and then your mind takes that sympathetic feeling and drains your energy with worry and sadness. Or you have expectations about yourself or others, but when those expectations are not met, your mind turns a disappointment into self-pity and starts to pout.

Sentimentality, attachment, sympathy, and expectation start as heartfelt expressions of care. Yet if you look deeper, you see how these attitudes can lead to overcare and much suffering, heartache, and depression.

While the core heart feeling of initial care is regenerative and uplifting, overcare is stress-inducing and draining. When you get the mind and heart back into coherent alignment, you can turn overcare back to real care and free yourself. Let's see how it works.

Sentimentality

Sentimentality starts with a sincere loving or caring feeling that ends up in sadness. When a tender feeling turns sentimental—like missing someone with whom you shared good times—the mental pictures and emotional memories create a sense of loss that can sink your heart into deep sorrow.

If you stay sentimental, it will cause a "bleeding heart." One sentimental emotion quickly attracts another, until before you know it, you're down in the dumps. The mind overidentifies with the memory—adding significance to what could have been—which ignites incoherence and sorrow, which ultimately degenerates into misery and depression. Managing sentiment isn't about cutting off the sad feeling or repressing it. By learning to recognize a *sentimental pull* toward sadness, you can bring the energy back to your heart and shift into coherence. Use the Quick Coherence technique so the deeper core values of your heart can be expressed. You honor your memories of other people by lifting sentiment into appreciation or compassion and understanding.

Appreciation is a quick way to bring in more of your real spirit. As you focus on the feeling of appreciation, your intuition can *clarify* more. Your thoughts and perspective will change. Heart intuition—not mind sentiment—is what will guide you to a new secure attitude that feels better to your real self. Often intuition comes as calming whisper thoughts that show you the direction to take. Even if you don't intuit an immediate direction, you'll rebuild your energy and sense of security.

Watch out for feelings of sentiment toward yourself too. If you are overweight and dwell on memories of when you could fit into smaller-sized clothes, that sentiment can turn to despair. It's not the memory itself, but the overattachment to what once was as well as the sense of failure that cause heartache and drain away your power. Dwelling on failure brings up more memories of past failures or parts of your life that are not working now. Brooding and lingering there will negate your self-worth and won't ever bring you any intuitive discernment.

As soon as you recognize sentimental thoughts taking over, use the Quick Coherence technique, find a feeling of appreciation for something in your life now, and enjoy that appreciative feeling for a few moments. This will bring you back to the present moment and start to restore your exhausted emotional power. It can also provide you with new perceptions on how to move forward.

Sympathy

Sympathy or sharing in another's sadness is tricky, because it seems like you are deeply caring. However, oversympathetic feelings actually diminish your intuition about how to help and reduce your ability to care. When your mind commiserates with another over their stress, it often projects more misery than is there. Before you know it, you are consumed and drained by sadness. Now there are two pitiful people instead of one.

Compassion is a core heart value that lifts you out of draining sympathy. Compassion balances care with understanding. You can feel what it's like to walk in other people's shoes but know when to stop—so you don't walk off a cliff with them!

A friend of ours once described the difference: "If someone's bucket has a hole in it, it doesn't help him [for you] to punch a hole in your own bucket."

Sympathy bleeds energy, while compassion gives you energy and provides insight on how to help. Notice when you are slipping into sympathy. You can feel it as a pull on your heartstrings or a heavy feeling in the pit of your stomach. Use Quick Coherence to lift your attention and energy into your heart and away from mind worries and fears that underlie sympathy. Breathe the heart feeling of appreciation and compassion for the person and for yourself in order to regain emotional balance.

Overattachment

Being overattached to anything saps your spirit and blocks the expression of your deeper values. It binds you to people, things, or ideas to the point that you lose perspective.

A mother has a natural feeling of attachment and love for her child. However, if she fusses over and spoils her child when they are together or frets every time they are apart, she reinforces insecurity in both of them and misses out on the richness of a deeper love. Healthy children naturally push away from overcaring and overattached parents. Overattachment seriously reduces the quality of love and leads to unhappiness.

Overattachment occurs when you are insecure and fear that you won't get your needs met. Your heart may need something other than what you think you want or ought to have. It is easy to mistake emotional desire for your real heart's desire.

When Diane was in college, she was fraught with overattachment to the idea of finding a romantic relationship. She compensated by overeating, swelling to fifty pounds above her normal weight in six months. To compensate for that, she became bulimic. Becoming overweight made her feel unattractive and added to her worries, so she ate more food. Overattachment can act as a continuous drain on your system, due to repetitive negative thoughts and attitudes that fuel your insecurity.

Managing desires with heart intelligence will help keep you from being blindsided by insecurities. Use the Quick Coherence technique when you feel pulled by a desire. It will build your strength to delay gratification until you are certain that you are following your real heart and not just an emotional pull.

Keep in mind that attachment to a particular outcome actually blocks the fulfillment you are hoping for. Fulfilling experiences will find you as you replace insecurity with balance and security.

Expectations

Everyone has expectations. You expect the sun to come up in the morning. You expect your family and friends to be pretty much the same tomorrow as they were yesterday. You expect yourself and those you care about to behave in certain ways. But the more attached you are to those expectations, the more disillusioned you will be if they aren't met. This is because you have an emotional investment in things going the way you want or think they should. That's not bad. It's only human.

Unmet expectations of wives, husbands, children, colleagues, mentors, and yourself are the source of most hurt and despair. Hope is lost as disappointment drains your emotional reserves.

Let's say you completed a project at work and are about to prepare a report on it. Holding an expectation that your boss or team will be as excited as you are could set you up for feeling devastated if they aren't. Approaching the report with a fun yet balanced expectancy—rather than an overattached expectation—will give you a lot more flexibility. It is better to deliver the report with sincerity, remain receptive to feedback, and maintain a sense of security. That way, whether your hopes and expectations are met or not, you can move forward without loss of energy.

High expectations lead to perfectionism and performance anxieties, which only perpetuate stress and can lead to depression. Stacey's story is a prime example of this.

Perfectionism runs in my family. Both of my parents have multiple graduate degrees from Ivy League schools. High performance was the air I breathed, so much a part of my upbringing that if someone had asked me if I was under any performance anxiety, I would not have known what they were talking about. Does a guppy in a lake know what water is?

When I was seven years old, my best friend was murdered in a violent crime. Shortly thereafter, both of my grandparents died suddenly. I went into a state of clinical depression.

For the next twenty years, I tried everything from psychotherapy to drugs to spiritual practices to try to overcome this monster I called my "black dog of depression." Each thing worked for a short time, giving me a teasing glance at what life would be like without a heavy weight pressing down on my chest. Then the inevitable return of overwhelm[ing feelings] and despair would slam me back into a state of powerless hopelessness.

I was repeatedly hospitalized for mysterious abdominal pain and unexplained menopause at the age of twenty. I dropped out of school, was desperately suicidal, had hot flashes and pain, and did not leave my parents' couch for months.

At twenty-two, I went on a Prozac derivative. The drug gave me a new lease on life. Even though I gained a lot of weight, couldn't sleep, and suffered memory loss as side effects, I did not mind. For the first time, I was free. But, like everything else I had tried, the antidepressant did not keep working.

In the middle of one week of winter exams, during which my performance anxiety was at a peak, my boyfriend broke up with me the same day the United States declared war on Iraq. I was filled with angst; confused about global politics, religion, and spirituality; living in a new place without friends or family nearby; and feeling like I had nowhere to turn.

My depression detonated. I remember standing on a cliff overlooking a freeway by the ocean, calculating the angle I would need to jump with to end my life. And then the irony struck me. I was on antidepressants and I wanted to kill myself. There was something funny about it, like, "Why take these? They are obviously not working!" Instead of throwing myself off the cliff, I cast out a prayer that I would find peace. Not temporary peace, but real and lasting peace, independent of circumstances.

Two weeks later I found myself volunteering at the Institute of HeartMath on my spring break from medical school. The job they gave me was to transcribe some of their research, in particular their research done on DHEA levels in perimenopausal women who had used their Cut-Thru technique. As I typed the physician's words into the computer, I kept thinking, "That's me! That's me! He is describing me exactly!"

With my medical background, it was very helpful to learn the science behind HeartMath while doing the transcriptions, in order to trust the process of the tools. For one thing, I was skeptical (since I had already tried so many other things). For another thing, I did not feel an emotional shift right away. I put aside any idealistic expectations and just practiced the tools.

It took about two weeks of sincere practice, without much result, before my depression truly lifted. Even more significantly, my early menopause symptoms went away and have not come back since. I've gone off medication entirely. My emotional state has continued to spiral up from there, as I have regularly used the HeartMath tools.

If Stacey could find benefit from the coherence-building tools, so can you. Simply practice them with genuine heart intent. If, like Stacey, you don't get results right away, just keep going. Don't let expectations stop you or blame the tools for not working or feel sorry for yourself and then give up. Realize that you are *building coherence* so it's not fair to yourself to expect a quick fix overnight. Instead, look for progress in steps and stages.

Feeling Sorry for Yourself

Feeling sorry for yourself often bottoms out in blame and self-pity. Self-pity saps your power and leaves you feeling flatter than a pancake. Self-pity bleeds so much energy that, after indulging in it, you can feel drained for days.

Self-pity is the opposite of compassionate understanding for yourself. You can notice the difference in your body. Compassion feels soothing and relaxing to the heart. It brings intuitive discernment that lets you see what can be improved, while self-pity creates an ache in the heart or pit of the stomach and sees no way out.

Left unchecked, self-pity becomes a chronic case of "poor me." This happens most often when you feel that someone—or life in general—hasn't been fair. You can drain your energy for days, weeks, months, or years by feeling sorry for yourself. Pretty soon you're feeling so sorry for yourself that all of life is tainted with despair. When self-pity or "poor me" occupies your mind, new possibilities simply can't get in and you're unable to take effective action.

Another expression of self-pity is *pout*. We've all seen young children turn out their lower lips and scowl when disappointed. Most of the time a child's pout doesn't last long. Children have more emotional flexibility than adults, so they don't tend to brood for days or weeks. They just pout until life offers a new opportunity, and then they move on—often in a matter of minutes.

In an adult, self-pity and pout can become ingrained habits that distort reality. When the mind habitually pouts, it misinterprets the communications and feelings of others. It programs and reprograms the hurt and resentment into the brain's neural circuitry, skewing the body's hormonal balance, depressing the immune system, and aging people before their time. Leaving the pouts unchecked or dramatizing them to prove a point can lead to depression and physical disorders.

Compassion and nonjudgment are absolutely essential to the process of releasing self-pity patterns. Hold yourself gently in the heart in a humble, open attitude of not knowing what's next or why things happened the way they did. Use the Quick Coherence technique to stop the self-pity and open your mind to new possibilities.

In the past few years, we have heard more stories than ever before of men and women who "have made it" careerwise or financially yet are suffering from an emptiness they can't seem to fill. A life of ambition in pursuit of money or career advancement did not deliver the emotional rewards or fulfillment that friends, family, and mentors had promised. They have the house, boat, spouse, children, job title, and money they strived so hard to get only to find they are left feeling hollow, dry. They are dejected from a loss of hope or loss of purpose.

> *One couple, Jerry and Ruth, went to a three-day retreat in Montana for executives like themselves who were suffering from depression. They realized they'd spent their lives living up to their own and others' expectations, and now that they had it all, they didn't know who they were.*
>
> *Jerry and Ruth so loved the quiet setting in the mountains and the other people who were also searching for answers that they didn't want to go back home. They could leave their old life behind them, move anywhere, and retire on their savings, but they didn't know where to go. So they didn't do anything. The old feelings of self-pity resurfaced as they went back to their previous life, because they couldn't see any way out.*

It's your mind adding significance, not your heart, that leads you down the road paved with good intentions into stress-induced depression. Love, care, appreciation, and compassion do not squelch hope. It is squelched when you allow these warmhearted feelings to become compromised by overcare, overidentity, and overattachment. You can realign your spirit, heart, mind, and emotions to change those old habits.

Understanding what creates stress-induced depression is the first step to taking back control of your life. The next step is practicing coherence-building tools to empower yourself to move forward.

Releasing overcare in even one area will often release overcare in other areas at the same time. This experience renews hope, and with hope comes a renewal of energy and passion for life.

chapter 6

The Power of Intent

As we've discussed in earlier chapters, many, many people are feeling out of control more of the time due to the increase of stressors in today's world. They are also becoming more sensitive to the influx of ongoing stress from wars, terror threats, social crises, political upsets, natural disasters, and so on. These ongoing stressors collectively create a stress wave and a static field of stress that affects people's nervous energy and clarity at work and at home. It's like a radio with so much static that even when you try to turn the knob, you can't find a clear station. This global-stress pulse wave has a blanket electromagnetic effect that causes people to overreact to things that didn't use to bother them as much. The static frequencies move through the collective consciousness, affecting energy levels and emotions. The result is more out-of-control feelings, like crying for no reason, panic attacks, or low-grade depression. People don't recognize where it is coming from. They just know that they feel a lot more stressed than they used to.

Feeling out of control makes people do whatever seems comforting—like eating or drinking too much. The stress creates an inertia that prevents people from changing attitudes or behaviors they know they should change or have been trying to change. It's one of the reasons people can feel lonely even when they are surrounded by family or friends. If this describes you at times, realize you are not alone. The static in the world creates a blanket of stress that everyone experiences unconsciously.

We feel it's important for people to understand this, so that they don't lose faith in themselves. This is why we spent so much time in chapter 5 addressing core heart feelings and values and how you can benefit from tapping into your deeper heart intentions.

Later in this chapter, you will learn another simple, yet powerful coherence-building technique: Attitude Breathing. Using replacement attitudes that bring you into increased coherence, the Attitude Breathing technique will help you fill your heart and act on your heart intelligence.

Keep in mind that it's harder to stick to a self-help program these days because of the stress on the planet. Practicing Attitude Breathing with heart intent will give you the alignment and empowerment to say, "I can do something about this." Instead of feeling mired in the stress around you, you will learn to take control of your stress response and change the reactions and behaviors that keep dragging you down. You can take back your power from the internal stresses that eat at you and build a new natural resistance to the influx of external stressors at home, at work, and in the world.

The Power of Heart Intent

Through increasing your coherence levels, meaningfulness can be added to heart intent to create the power needed to release deep emotional resistances and stress.

Heart intent is not merely willpower or mind-focused intent. It is far more solid than willpower alone and has more staying power. You can apply willpower to your mind's intentions and achieve certain results. For instance, suppose you were going to clean your carpet, but you kept putting it off until finally you put your mind to it and did it. That's fine for cleaning carpets, but willpower and mind intent are not enough to clear disturbed emotions that keep coming back. That requires a different power of intent that has to be pulled out of the heart.

Mental determination won't change emotional energies that can haunt you. If you are harboring emotions about incidents in the past that felt unfair and caused you pain and disappointment, no amount of mental determination can give you relief. However, meaningful intent from the heart can transform emotional storage banks of despair, hopelessness, and other painful emotions.

Resignation

When people begin to recognize that willpower and mental intent won't work to release their distress, many slide into feelings of resignation. Resignation is like a set of stairs going down toward depression. If you think you may be experiencing a sense of resignation, look for these signposts: you have attitudes of "I just don't care anymore," "things will never change," and "life is unfair." Once these attitudes take hold, you start to go down the stairs. You spend more time alone and cut yourself off from activities and people; you feel there's a dampener between you and close friends or family members; you find the things that used to interest and inspire you now seem dull and dry; and you feel like a robot going through the motions of living. As the positive emotional textures of life become muted, mental confusion and depression set in. If you allow resignation to have a chronic place in your life, you are also putting your health at risk.

So much resignation can be prevented by having the meaningful heart intent and commitment to clear unresolved feelings as you go and before they get stored. That's how you start to transform depression. If you haven't cleared something that's festering, then make a commitment to use the heart tools to clear them.

Understanding Your Rhythms

Everyone's mental, emotional, and physical energies operate in different rhythms throughout the month. Once you understand that these rhythms move in cycles and waves, you can know when it's time to increase your practice of the heart tools to help offset down rhythms and to bring your nervous and hormonal systems back into balance.

One of the first things to do is to notice the difference when your energy gets overamped or runs at a lower keel at different times during a day, week, or month. These are important hinge points.

When you get overamped, you tend to overreact. When your energy is at a lower keel, you can tend to get stuck in the same old mental, emotional, or physical habits. At these hinge points, using the tools will play an even more important part in your practice.

If you stay diligent with the tools during those times, it will keep your flexibility up so you don't get as thrown by stressors. When your natural rhythms aren't up to par, you may be more prone to irritation at work or frustration with the kids or impatience in traffic. You may also be more prone to feeling anxiety or despair about your appearance, your health, or your future.

Because of standard rhythms your emotions go through, it's easy to miss these hinge points and revert back to ineffective and habitual reactions to events in life (see the section Hinge Points in chapter 3). Using the tools at those hinge points will break this cycle and keep you on a forward momentum.

For example, statistics show that even when you're off and running with good momentum, the full moon can increase emotional reactivity. Your mind can get overamped, and you can think the worst about everything. This makes problems suddenly look bigger than life. To avoid this, remember to use the tools more often during the few days before and after the full moon to increase your balance and flexibility. Negative thinking and impulsive choices are much more likely when you don't have the emotional flexibility to resist them.

Anything that drains your emotional energy reduces your flexibility and saps your commitment to follow your heart intentions. Each round of stress you cave in to makes you more vulnerable to old mental persuasions and emotional pulls that can start a downward spiral to resignation and hopelessness.

Guilt can also start the spiral. Caving in to guilt leads to resignation, an attitude of "I don't care anymore," and then to feelings of hopelessness. Use the tools to help rid yourself of any guilt and get right back on your practice program. It's critical to stop the thoughts of "I'm bad" when guilt starts. Judging yourself as someone who is bad creates a type of energy drain that builds a subconscious resignation that's hard to pull out of, causing despair and a sense of failure. Instead, you can track your rhythms and renew your heart commitment to using the tools at those critical times and stop a downward spiral in its tracks.

Tracking Your Rhythms

Write down the times of a day, week, and month when your emotions tend to get overamped or run at a low keel. Note how these rhythms affect your attitudes and how you tend to react. By tracking your rhythms (writing them down), you will learn to identify the hinge points. Make a commitment to use the tools with a deeper heart intent at those times, right when those predictable triggers start to show up and get in your way.

People have different emotional and hormonal rhythms during a month, times when insecurities can become more amplified. Once insecurities get amplified, that diminishes all types of commitments you need to maintain your well-being: diet, exercise, honest communication, and so forth. Insecurities can leave you much more vulnerable to anything that can cause you to veer from the important intentions you have.

Don't stop using the heart tools. Using your tools at these times, especially, will help you reconnect with your inner security and snap back to your commitment.

Getting Back on Track—How to Handle a Spinout

If a trying situation gets you to overreact or spin out of control, just use the tools to get right back on track. Be sure to use the tools when a family member or business disturbance causes an emotional dropout—meaning that you're brooding over what happened and not present to what's going on around you. Mental and emotional brooding is a sign that it's time to grab a heart tool so you stop draining energy.

Pre-treatment

Once you track your rhythms, you can begin to *pre-treat* them. Attitude Breathing is a powerful pre-treatment tool. You prepare your attitude before engaging in situations that are likely to cause you to overreact. You use Attitude Breathing before the wave hits. It will help you maintain your commitment and ride the emotional wave if it comes.

Attitude Breathing also helps to progressively diminish insecurities as you build more coherence and confidence. For example, suppose you have a rebellious teenager who doesn't listen to what you're saying. You're preparing to talk to him, but you know it's going to be a problem. Use Attitude Breathing before the talk to pre-treat yourself and your attitude so you can keep your balance during the talk. Keep using Attitude Breathing during the conversation—along with Notice and Ease, Power of Neutral, and Quick Coherence. (You may need all of them—especially if your teenager acts out!)

Pre-treating stressful situations before they happen will help cue up your commitments to use Notice and Ease, Power of Neutral, Quick Coherence, and Attitude Breathing. You will be ahead of the curve and able to shift your energetics to ride the emotional wave with more coherence and balance.

✐ Attitude Breathing Technique

Step 1. Recognize an unwanted attitude—a feeling or attitude that you want to change. This could be anxiety, sadness, despair, depression, self-judgment, guilt, anger, feeling overwhelmed—anything that's distressing.

Step 2. Identify and breathe in a replacement attitude: select a positive attitude and then breathe the feeling of that new attitude in slowly and casually through your heart area. Do this for a while to anchor the new feeling.

Unwanted Feelings/Attitudes	Examples of Replacement Feelings/Attitudes
stress	Breathe neutral to chill out and revitalize.
anxiety	Breathe calm and balance.
feeling overwhelmed	Breathe ease and peace.
sadness or depression	Breathe appreciation and nonjudgment.
guilt	Breathe compassion and nonjudgment.

As you breathe these replacement attitudes, tell yourself to take the "big deal" and drama out of the negative feeling or attitude. Tell yourself, "Take the significance out." Repeat this over and over as you use Attitude Breathing until you feel a shift or a change. Remember that even when a negative attitude feels justified, the buildup of negative emotional energy will block up your system. Have a genuine "I mean business" attitude and heart intent to really move those emotions into a more coherent state. It could take a few minutes of Attitude Breathing, but it's worth the practice.

Start with the attitude replacement list above and be open to a new replacement attitude from your heart intuition. If you are worried, breathe calm; but remember—this requires breathing the attitude of calm until you actually *feel* more calmed. That's when you have made what we call an *internal energetic shift*. This means that the turbulent emotional energy in your subconscious has shifted. Keep breathing the feeling of the new attitude to make it more real.

Note which replacement attitudes or core heart feelings give you the most relief when you practice Attitude Breathing, and write them down. Keep practicing those and then try Attitude Breathing with other attitude replacements.

Replacement attitudes need to be practical. You don't want to pick an idealistic replacement attitude. For example, you wouldn't want to say, "I feel sad and depressed, so I'm going to breathe happiness and joy." You probably won't be able to make a leap to feeling joy and happiness, and, if you think you are supposed to, it will only leave you feeling discouraged. Instead, you could say, "I feel sad and depressed, so I'm going to breathe appreciation [for something you like] and nonjudgment [about whatever is causing the sadness or depression]." As you practice the replacement attitudes from the list, stay open to new replacement attitudes from your heart intuition and add those to your practice.

Obstinacy

Obstinacy indicates a "stuck" attitude. Obstinacy arises when you *just know* something was or is the way you see it. You won't consider the possibility that your belief may not be accurate or that there may be a larger view that you can't yet perceive. You may hold on to obstinacy in the name of a principle, even though it keeps causing you hurt, pain, or grief. Your intelligence knows better, but you can't seem to stop the feelings or thoughts. Obstinacy is also in place when there are things you know you need to do, but you don't do them. If you stay obstinate long enough, that negative attitude turns into an ingrained or stuck feeling in your unconscious that can feel like a cement block around your heart.

Negative attitudes also generate emotional undercurrents that seem to always be there, like a background noise, affecting your mood swings, your feelings overall, and your relationships. By learning to activate warmhearted feelings that generate heart rhythm coherence, you can start to release those negative undercurrents and incoherent feelings. Everybody has some of these, so they're not bad. They're just old stored patterns. The Attitude Breathing tool is designed to help you clear negative attitudes and obstinate stuck feelings by making the energetic shift that will bring you new perspectives.

Making the Energetic Shift

An attitude shift is the first step toward an *energetic shift*. If you can't make a mental attitude shift with Attitude Breathing, see if you can find the resignation or obstinacy that's causing you to hold on to a negative attitude. Once you have the heart intention to make an attitude shift and mean business about adopting a replacement attitude, it can be harder at first to find the *feeling* of that attitude. This is especially so if you have been depressed for a while.

If you have a hard time feeling appreciation, for example, start by breathing *nonjudgment* and *calm* as replacement attitudes. Next, find a memory associated with a feeling of inner calm, while sustaining your heart focus. Once you find some benefit from breathing calm, start to appreciate the calm. Breathe appreciation for feeling calmer, and you will begin to find a feeling of appreciation. Continue to breathe appreciation for whatever benefit you are experiencing and breathe nonjudgment toward whatever hasn't yet released.

If your feelings are still stuck, use the other tools you've learned so far to help you make the energetic shift. Use Notice and Ease and Power of Neutral to help you observe your mind and emotions. Use Quick Coherence to increase coherence and heart alignment. Then go back to Attitude Breathing.

Try breathing an attitude of compassion or forgiveness or try befriending the feelings as a replacement. Remember to breathe slowly and casually, and stay focused on the replacement even if you still feel resistance. Imagine pulling in and anchoring those replacement feelings in the heart. As you keep practicing, you will start to create new neural pathways and make the energetic shift where resistance and obstinacy progressively release.

Befriending Negative Attitudes and Stuck Feelings

Attitude Breathing doesn't deny or repress negative attitudes or resistant feelings. Instead, it helps transform them. This is important to understand. You are actually *befriending* a negative attitude or feeling by bringing that blocked energy into your heart, not fighting it but holding it in your heart and releasing the significance you've assigned to it.

Negative attitudes and emotions aren't bad, as we've said before. They are a completely understandable result of past situations that have caused you hurt or pain. But that doesn't mean you can't change the ratio of how much low-grade negativity and judgment you carry around and experience now. Your heart can open you to new information and insight that transforms your view of the past and releases resistant feelings. You can develop the heart intelligence to clear out a lot of stored negativity that keeps triggering depression. As you practice attitude replacements to clear negativity, the triggers will come up with less energy and have less cumulative long-range effect.

It takes meaningful heart intent to release stored negativity—a deep yet accessible intent. Ellen's story, sent to us by a health professional, shows how meaningful heart intent works, even when someone is in chronic pain.

My problem with chronic pain began about eight years ago. I developed back and right-leg pain from a work-related injury and had surgery to correct a disk problem. The surgery was "successful," but my pain never improved. My emotional state began to worsen. After my second surgery I couldn't walk; I could barely stand up. I was given twenty-four visits with a physical therapist, but that was not enough.

I never really improved over the years, even though I had occasional physical therapy, acupuncture, and psychotherapy. Besides that, all I was offered for such a long time was a bunch of pills or an epidural shot. I couldn't sit up in bed or stand up from a chair without a pulley or assistance. I felt so lonesome, useless, and worthless. I had gained weight because I was feeling "What's the point—life's not worth living, if this is the way it's going to be." I was feeling worse and worse, like I was just taking up space.

After waiting for a long time, I finally heard that I was eligible for a new pain-management program and I cried the whole day. I was scared. I hoped my body wouldn't let me down. I wanted to come out as a human being again. The best thing that could have happened to me was that program. I was introduced to HeartMath, and it was wonderful. HeartMath taught me that I could handle my pain and depression. I learned that it takes practice and a willingness to keep trying, but it can be managed.

I've really needed to use the [Power of] Neutral tool when situations around me or my pain gets challenging. Sometimes my knee gets so bad that I almost fall, and I get angry. Then I tell myself, "Before you get all upset, just get in that Neutral Place." Then I can shift focus to the positive. I can Attitude Breathe and deal with it then.

I'm going to have a total knee replacement soon and will have a brand-new knee. My depression level is almost nonexistent now. I just don't feed into it. I act before it takes hold of me—when I feel it coming on. I use HeartMath tools to find a positive outlook. Without them, I probably wouldn't have been able to deal with all the stress and pain.

I'm not taking any pills anymore (except for blood pressure and thyroid). I'm off Soma, Vicodin, Neurontin, Keppra, Topamax, and Cymbalta. I'd be taking something, if not for HeartMath. I found my attitude changed after I started using it. It gave me a focus.

Yes, life has sent me some curveballs, and my pain probably won't ever totally go away, but you have to take control of you— your feelings, your pain—and not let it control you. I talk to my pain: "I'm not focusing on you today." It works. I've expanded on feeling heart feelings to doing things I enjoy. Now I'll be singing, dancing, and moving every body part that I can while I do my heart tools. My leg will still be hurting, but I move every part that I can move. It helps to really feel better.

The other day, I saw the psychologist I've been seeing for several years and he said, "You've got your cane, but you're swinging it!"

In the next few chapters, you will learn two more powerful techniques to help you clear stored negative emotional energy. The Heart Lock-In technique will help you sustain coherence for longer periods to promote healing. The Cut-Thru technique will help you clear deeper emotional issues and reinforce the new neural pathways and attitudes you are building.

chapter 7

Putting a Stop to Fatigue

How well you manage your attitudes and emotions each day determines to a large extent how much vitality you will experience overall. Most people think fatigue sets in because of all the things they have to do or because they didn't get enough sleep. They often overlook the energy drain from out-of-control emotions.

Different triggers in life can cause stress to run through your system, creating frayed nerves, fatigue, and overwhelming, out-of-control feelings. Once this occurs, it's important to recover from the stress fast, otherwise your energy drains away. Taking emotional responsibility to get into heart rhythm coherence helps to rebalance your system. Coherence also helps you develop the intuitive discernment to see how to stop draining energy and renew your vitality. This is especially important when you are trying to lift depression.

When you have plenty of energy and you're on a roll (feeling like you're moving in a smooth flow), you carry a certain energetic presence. But then on those days where something triggers anger or blame, you can feel your energy dip. And then there are those days where the fritterings of anxious inner dialogue, pouting, or emotional insecurities allow your energy to leak all day like a dripping faucet. You may not notice or understand the impact that these very private mental and emotional energy expenditures have on your vitality, but they are a constant drain.

Why Sleep Isn't Enough

Each night you sleep to rest the mind and body from the previous day's concerns and to recoup the energy spent. Lots of people skimp on sleep due to the pressure of having so many things to do. Many sleep fitfully due to worries and anxieties they can't shut off. Everyday concerns drain their energy much of the night, and then they drag themselves through the next day wondering why life feels so hard. The greatest cause of low vitality and ongoing fatigue is this emotional and mental unrest. People need sleep just to rest from their negative thoughts and feelings. The irony is that sleep gives them just enough energy so they can do the same thing over again the next day and the next—drain their energy away in anxiety, judging, and blame.

Sleeplessness and insomnia have become acute problems for seventy million people in the United States alone, according to the National Center on Sleep Disorders Research. The health consequences add about $15 billion to the national health care bill and cost industry $50 billion in lost productivity. The National Highway Traffic Safety Administration estimates that about 56,000 automobile accidents per year are the result of drivers falling asleep at the wheel.

If you are experiencing crippling fatigue—especially if it accompanies other unexplainable symptoms, like memory impairment or muscle pain—it's important to consult a physician. Clinical illnesses, such as sleep apnea or chronic fatigue and immune dysfunction syndrome (CFIDS), may have different causes than the exhaustion that results from the wear and tear of everyday life. But even clinical illnesses are made worse from the drain of unmanaged emotions.

Just as you can drain energy like a sieve by not managing your emotions, so you can accumulate energy quickly through just a little emotional management. You reaccumulate emotional energy each time you use one of the heart coherence tools. You need to fill your tank of emotional energy to lift depression. When you practice the tools, you give your system a chance to build up your *emotional accumulators*. Your cells accumulate and store emotional energy, just as they store physical energy. That's how you can feel buoyant or emotionally renewed at times. Heart coherence starts emotional regeneration. It's like an activator that helps you deal more effectively with whatever is challenging you.

In fact, the deepest form of rest, recuperation, and regeneration is heart rhythm coherence. When you are in a deep sleep, your heart rhythms naturally go into the coherence mode. The smooth, sine-wavelike pattern of heart rhythm coherence is the mode the body naturally slips into during deep, restorative sleep. You will learn the Heart Lock-In technique later in this chapter to help you lock in and sustain heart rhythm coherence for longer periods.

Rebuilding Your Emotional Accumulators

Emotional energy provides the firepower for carrying out your intentions. Having a full tank of positive emotional energy is important to achieving success in any area. It boosts your mental clarity and intuitive discernment ability. You can't think as well when your emotional energy accumulators are drained. When your emotional energy accumulators are low, you have poor or unregulated nervous system activity, which decreases vitality, discernment, and the ability to make good decisions.

The *bioelectric system* (nervous system and cells) of each human being absorbs, accumulates, and discharges energy (physical, emotional, mental, and spiritual). Emotional energy is the fuel for smooth mental processes—it provides consistent energy to handle the inevitable "glitches" in life. That's why people often say "Let's sleep on it" when their energy is low. They know that they cannot make the best decisions when they feel incoherent or fatigued.

You may use exercise or meditation to rebuild your energy accumulators, but if a lot of that time is spent rehashing your worries or judgments, then you are draining energy while trying to accumulate it.

Some people have more stress triggers to deal with than others. As a result, they have a higher potential drain ratio. Think of police, schoolteachers, or single parents, juggling very demanding jobs with children, housework, and more bills than they can afford to pay. For many, having these stressors isn't a choice—but they still always have a choice in how to emotionally manage them.

It's not the stressors themselves that drain you, but how you emotionally respond to them. You can drain energy by trying to "do good" and wear yourself out. But you can also build your way into an *independence zone*. You will rebuild your emotional accumulators as you begin to identify what drains you, then use heart coherence tools to stop those draining mental and emotional reactions.

✐ *Identify What Drains You*

Start to observe the modulations in your energy throughout the day. Ask yourself periodically, "Am I gaining or draining?"

Make notes of the times, circumstances, and emotional responses that give you energy gains. Make the same kind of notes when you notice energy drains. Keep a log of your energy gains and drains for a few days. Use the heart tools and techniques you've learned to prep for potential drain times and to reduce the time it takes to recover afterwards. If there are certain times of the day, like four o'clock in the afternoon, when you notice your energy starts to fade or you tend to be more irritable, plan a break or some other restorative activity at that time. Take a ten-minute walk, use a heart tool, eat a nourishing snack, or talk to someone to improve your attitude and recharge your batteries.

Your bioelectric system has tides of energy and natural rhythms that flow through it during the course of a week or a month. As your heart awareness increases, you'll be able to discern when your physical rhythms are low and you need to slow down a bit. You'll recognize when your emotions are more sensitive and you need to be gentler with yourself, or when your mind needs a break before you can think clearly again. You will also be able to tell the difference between tiredness caused by low ebbs in the tide and the kind of fatigue you feel even at high tide because your mental or emotional energy is getting drained away through lack of self-management.

Stay in a Soft Heart

It's natural to not feel good or to feel down at times. The best thing to do is to move in what we call a *soft heart*, which is a balancing place to regenerate as you go. A soft heart isn't something mushy. It's an easygoing, warm place in the heart.

Assign your thoughts, feelings, and energies to "soak" in a soft-heart attitude while you do casual work for a while. Keeping your energies in a soft heart can allow more coherent rhythms to emerge, which help you recoup mental, emotional, and physical vitality. At times, physical exercise or a brisk walk in fresh air can bring the change of pace needed for recharge and balance.

If you suffer from chronically low vitality or fatigue, keep a piece of paper by your side and write down your energy gains and drains for a week or longer. See what rhythms or patterns emerge, and ask your heart intuition what adjustments to make in attitude, diet, exercise, and so on. Making adjustments won't be easy if you anxiously compare yourself to others, thinking, "Well, they always seem to be bubbling along. Maybe they don't have as much on their plate as I do" or "I have to keep going to keep up or I'll look bad." These attitudes devitalize and drain you even more. They increase the down time and make it harder to find the regenerative soft-heart place.

It takes respect for yourself to depersonalize whatever's going on and stay in a soft heart to recoup energy. Take the significance out of situations and what others might think. It may be as simple as reminding yourself that you are tired and may not be seeing clearly. Use the Power of Neutral tool and sincerely rest in the soft heart. If you move in slower motion for a bit, you will find your emotional energy delicately recharges, and eventually your vitality and heart buoyancy will return. Once your energy renews, ask your heart intelligence to alert you when your mind triggers on something and starts to drain you again. Then you will be able to use a tool to plug the drain before it runs you down.

Kate describes how the tools helped her:

Using these heart tools has been most powerful for me in dealing with low energy and times I wasn't feeling well.

It all started when, for a few weeks, I felt fatigued, and sleep wouldn't cure it. All my life I've been a go-getter, pushing on through projects and being the last person to drop, so this was unusual for me. I started asking my heart intuition to show me when to go to soft heart before speaking or reacting to people's comments or actions. When I wasn't aligned with the heart, everything made me irritable. I had some great days and a few gray moments.

Then I came down with the flu. I don't get sick or miss work often, but I had to surrender and just lie in bed and sleep. Going to my soft heart helped me to find a very peaceful state that allowed me a feeling of regeneration I had not felt before.

I decided to look at the sick time as a vacation. I couldn't feel the flu bug unless my mind started thinking I was sick. Then my fever would rise, and my head would start to hint at a headache. So I asked myself why I would choose to think "sick" over feeling like I was on vacation.

Once I was back on my feet, the feeling of my experience remained. In my day-to-day relationships—personal and work—I knew that I had to treat all like I did the flu. I moved slower, respecting my energies, maintaining the regeneration of my "sick-vacation" time. I actually got more done with less time wasted, and that surprised me.

In retrospect, I can see that getting sick was a blessing. It slowed me down and gave me the opportunity to see how I had been causing low energy and fatigue. I know I don't need to push anything and can ease into things, speak my truth sincerely and with care, listen to my heart, and act on what it's telling me.

Kate emerged a stronger, more mature person from being sick. As valuable as her lessons were, Kate would be the first to admit that it is even better to learn them without waiting for tiredness and fatigue to turn into sickness. As soon as you notice the feeling of fatigue setting in, it's time to take action to rebuild your emotional energy accumulators.

Use the Heart Lock-In Technique

The Heart Lock-In technique is designed to help you rebuild your emotional energy accumulators (especially after they've been drained) and sustain coherence for longer periods of time. It will also help you instate, or lock in, new attitudes. During a Heart Lock-In, you generate in yourself a positive energy of appreciation and caring and send or radiate that energy to yourself and others, changing the energetic environment within and around you.

Most people find that practicing the Heart Lock-In technique for five minutes or longer, a couple of times a day, helps accumulate energy and recharge their emotional system. This cushions the impact of day-to-day stressors. It helps them maintain focus and see more clearly how to stop energy drains and make better decisions.

Heart Lock-In Technique

Step 1. Shift your attention to the area of your heart, and breathe slowly and deeply.

Step 2. Activate and sustain a genuine feeling of appreciation or care for someone or something in your life.

Step 3. Send these feelings of care toward yourself and others. This benefits them and especially helps recharge and balance your own system.

If your mind starts wandering during a Heart Lock-In, simply refocus your attention on the heart area and reconnect with your real love, care, or appreciation for someone. As you keep pulling your attention back to the heart, you build power to stay in coherence. When you experience heavy, uncomfortable, or stuck feelings during a Heart Lock-In, don't worry. Just send care or compassion to befriend those feelings.

You may not even know why a heavy or stuck feeling is there. That's standard until you unlock the emotional history underlying it. Befriending the feeling and sending compassion can help release a blockage. Resistant feelings often come and go and are released gradually as you gain more intuition about them. After practicing Heart Lock-In, write down intuitive ideas that you'd like to remember to act on. Practicing Heart Lock-In helps you stop judging, blaming, and worrying. It helps build courage to carry out your heart intentions.

One of the most effective times to practice Heart Lock-In is first thing in the morning before all the activity starts, to set the tone for your day. You'll stay more coherent in the midst of typical stressors, like getting ready for work, getting the kids off to school, dealing with traffic, and other challenging situations. A morning Heart Lock-In also puts fuel in your tank to power up your use of the heart tools during the day to manage your emotions, stay flexible, and shift back to coherence faster.

Doing a midday Heart Lock-In for five minutes is very effective for offsetting afternoon drag and reenergizing your emotional system. Afternoon drag causes less presence and low motivation that can lead to emotional reactivity. Another important time to use Heart Lock-In is before bed to promote deeper, more restful sleep.

Practicing Heart Lock-In brings in more of your spirit to help create alignment and coherence between your heart, emotions, mind, body, and spirit. The more you sustain the heart rhythm coherence mode, the easier it is for your brain's neural circuits to begin functioning from a healthier baseline. Heart Lock-In powers up your entire system to help you transform depression.

Creating Energetic Presence

Fatigue has become a huge issue in today's world. Your sincere efforts to maintain heart awareness will help you to stay conscious of your energy levels and to make needed adjustments to sustain your vitality. This energetic presence is needed, or you'll miss or ignore the signals the heart is sending you. When presence is low, the heart can tell you to do one thing, but you go the other way because you're not present enough to hear it or pay attention to it. Maintaining presence means you are more able to hear your heart's intuition in the moment and act on it. Then you won't slip too far into an energy drain.

Low energy and ongoing fatigue often lead to depression, and depression often perpetuates fatigue and low energy. In the end, heart awareness and energetic presence is what gives you the power to rebuild your emotional accumulators and lift depression. Heart awareness is where you connect with the power of your spirit and where you have the most intelligent control over your body's neurochemistry.

One of the greatest contributors to fatigue and depression is blame. Blaming a boss who makes unreasonable demands or an impossible family member or your overloaded life will only drain you. Blaming yourself for your shortcomings will also drain you. Emotional energy drain from blame results in diminished presence. Rather than being fully present in your own life, you're only half there.

Being mentally, emotionally, and physically present means staying in the heart of the moment. Businesses today talk about "presenteeism" as a measure of productivity. Mistakes are made, communications missed, and time lost when people are physically present but mentally and emotionally absent. One of the main causes of presenteeism is mental and emotional preoccupation with worry and blame.

In another sense of the word, people often focus on how they "present" themselves—the way they appear, what they wear, what they say, what car they drive—without realizing how much anxiety and energy drain they cause themselves over those things. When we introduce the HeartMath programs to companies, we explain to participants that "if you put a fraction of your energy into how you *present yourself to yourself* on mental and emotional levels, you will see where you are draining energy. Then you can use the tools to plug the leaks and automatically increase your presence."

Vitality renews as you are able to sustain presence. When your presence dims, your heart signals you to stop and do something different to recharge, if you listen to it. The mind tends to want to push on, find some distracting stimulation, or look for something or someone to complain about instead of looking within to what attitude or perception might be causing the brownout.

When people use a flashlight and it starts to go dim, the first thing they do is shake it to try to get the electrical connection back. If that doesn't work, they open it up and check the batteries. When their personal presence dims because their internal batteries are run down, they probably don't think about the electrical connection inside or about how to recharge their batteries. Instead they tend to get cranky and look for someone or something to take it out on. Young children do that, but so do adults.

Car batteries can drain too, but no one blames the next car over in the parking lot. Human beings don't tend to respect their system's energy needs the way they respect the simple mechanical operations of a flashlight or a car. Blame only perpetuates drain.

Once you let blame get to a certain point of intensity, it flings open the door to other draining attitudes, such as feeling sorry for yourself or wallowing in self-pity until you're depressed. Once your ability to be present drops below a certain point, only a jump start will build you back up to a basic operating level where you feel everything's all right. But even then, you haven't made it to feeling full of vitality.

Car batteries diminish more rapidly when there's a break-down in the generator or alternator. Once you understand that your heart is your generator bringing in your real spirit to keep your internal batteries continuously recharged, then you will want to attend to your heart more regularly. Living more presently in each moment, being in touch with your heart awareness, keeps your generator humming and your batteries charged.

Living in the Now

When people are fatigued, they long for some peace and quiet. Most feel that peace and quiet is something they have to go somewhere else to get. What they don't realize is that each time you listen to your heart intelligence, you are creating an inner compartment of stored peace and quiet.

You can accumulate peace and quiet—in this moment and then the next—by listening to your heart and making attitude adjustments as you go. That's emotional management through heart intelligence. The buoyancy that comes from accumulating peace and quiet brings in transformative energy, presence, and intuitive understanding of how to do things differently, even during difficult circumstances. It takes presence to connect with that intuitive heart discernment.

Tiredness should be a natural state occurring after a long day's work, a strenuous physical workout, or an illness. When you're recovering from flu, people naturally say "take it easy for a while." Maybe after a full day's work and before an upcoming meeting that night, a half-hour nap might be the best thing you could do to recharge your batteries.

As you listen to your heart's intuition and rhythms, you maximize your energy output by building in short recharge times between active times. People used to do this naturally when life was less hectic. Now that the pace is faster, they need to consult their heart intelligence even more.

Heart intelligence can take the burrs and spurs out of your feeling world during the day. This is energy saved, which furthers emotional ease and presence. Your energy by day will be more vital and your sleep at night more rewarding and peaceful. As you regain emotional flexibility, you will start to reexperience the peaceful tiredness you knew as a child and renew energy more fully as you sleep.

Halley had exhausted herself under such chronic stress for so long without realizing it that she could barely remember what it felt like to have that kind of peaceful tiredness at the end of a long day. Her tension and fatigue had built up to such an extent that she could no longer find the energy to reach her goals in life, much less experience the joy and contentment she used to feel. She knew something was wrong.

That's when I was given the basic tools of HeartMath, including the Heart Lock-In. In a short time, I couldn't believe how [different I] felt! I began to feel excitement for life again. I started to trust that my life did have meaning

*and that I could tap into my own unique manifestation of
purpose. I became the source of my own empowerment.*

*Not only did my depression shift as I used the tools
regularly, but the youthful passion and inspiration I longed
for in life came back. The beauty of this experience is that not
only do I have the joy and interest back in my life, but I have
learned the tools to bring it in at will.*

As you use the heart tools and techniques, you will learn
to recharge your batteries as you go. Situations that throw you
off balance when your energy is low—causing you to feel more
anxiety, sadness, or blame—won't have the same impact. You'll
stay in the flow longer, which is regenerative in itself, because
flow is a most efficient use of energy.

Learn to focus in your heart periodically throughout each
day, becoming more present to yourself. Gather your mental,
emotional, and physical energies in your heart and relax them
there. Put down your pen, stop fidgeting or multitasking, and
be present. It only will take a minute or two.

Ask your heart to get your batteries in line—physical,
mental, emotional, and spiritual. *Live in the now*—in this
moment. Let your heart intuition guide you to what adjustments, if any, you need to make in attitude or activity to
rebuild your energy. Then the flashlight that is you will shift
to a brighter beam—your highest potential in each moment.

chapter 8

Lifting Longer-Term Depression

People experience different types of depression. For some, recurring depressive episodes last a few hours or a few days. For others, periods of depression can last weeks, months, or even years.

Traumatic events often topple people into depression. This can happen because your sense of identity is deeply threatened or shattered. Trauma from heartbreak, betrayal, or violation can devastate your self-image and self-worth, causing a depressive loop.

Self-worth issues often feed longer-term depression, whether or not you have had emotional trauma. Ongoing judging of others or self-blaming thoughts and attitudes reinforce each other until they become automatic and take you down into a funk. Then you can get into another mental and emotional loop trying to release the funk, which acts like quicksand, trapping you in feelings of emotional density. The looping thoughts and feelings keep seeping back in, even while you're thinking about things that should make you happy. That's because of the emotional significance and overidentity you've invested in those looping thoughts and feelings over time.

The word "depression" means "low in spirit" or "dispirited." It literally describes your spirit in a bogged-down or blocked state.

When people aren't in alignment with their deeper heart, spirit can't flow in, and they tend to experience a feeling of compression. Some feel the compression around the heart area. Some feel the weight of the world is on their shoulders, and others feel disoriented. If the feeling of compression persists, it will manifest in biological imbalances eventually, whether in nervous system, neurotransmitter, or hormonal imbalances.

If you don't address compression, you can slide into a full-blown temporary or long-term depression. The most common phases of depression show a gradual slide into more serious problems:

- accumulated mental and emotional funk

- lack of spirit impression (spirit can't flow in)

- compression

- biological imbalances

- temporary or long-term depression

Lifting depression requires a download of spirit. The quickest way to invite more of your spirit in is through increasing heart rhythm coherence. Heart coherence realigns the brain and nervous system with your heart and spirit.

Overidentity That Leads
to Depression

A chronic overidentity with another person, issue, or situation will almost inevitably end up in disappointment that can start the downward spiral into depression. This is because your happiness is invested in something outside yourself rather than your internal resources. Your inner resources are always available to you when you need them. You cannot say the same for things outside of yourself.

This is what happened to Kelly. She was happily married to a successful businessman. They had a beautiful son and were leading what she thought was a comfortable life, when she discovered that her husband was having an affair. It came as a total shock. When Kelly confronted her husband, he left her and moved in with his girlfriend. Kelly was devastated. Not long afterwards, he filed for divorce and married the woman he had been having an affair with. Kelly's sense of self-worth and her net worth were both shattered. She went into deep depression.

The positive identity she had taken from something outside herself—her marriage and her assumptions about her life—suddenly turned into a negative identity. Negative identity leads to narrow, pessimistic thinking, which confirms and feeds energetic investment in a depressed mood. Negative thinking and a depressed mood keep feeding one another in an endless loop. Kelly couldn't break the circuit, so the feedback loop intensified into ever-worsening dark moods and deep depression.

Even with drug therapy and psychotherapy, she experienced recurring cycles of depression. Every few months she'd spiral downward and for three or four days couldn't get out of bed. Finally the depression would lift enough that she could pull herself out of it and go back to work. This cycling continued on and off for many years. She was prescribed MAO inhibitors and serotonin reuptake inhibitors. The drugs made her less depressed, but she felt no joy in life either. She said the drugs cut off feelings in her heart, so she didn't want to take them anymore.

Drug therapy may provide a much-needed biochemical lift for a while. It may help renew energy and motivation for doing the psychological work on what caused a depression in the first place. But that psychological work has to be done. Drugs alone rarely do the trick. They may reduce unhappiness, but they probably won't make you happy. Genuine happiness is a natural, resilient state you feel once you free the heart from the burdens of overidentity and depressive loops. Since depression is usually the culmination of succumbing to well-worn negative emotional and mental patterning, the inner work can't be ignored.

Drugs do not cure depression. Drugs alter brain states, which, in some people, masks or relieves depressive symptoms for a while. Some drugs are stimulants or sedatives and some blunt feelings, but none have been proven to bring long-term mood elevation or clear the cause of depression (Moncrieff and Cohen 2006).

Cutting Through the Feedback Loop

Recently, a research breakthrough occurred when Dr. Helen Mayberg identified an area of the brain, which scientists call Area 25, as a key conduit of neural traffic between the brain's thinking centers (in the frontal cortex) and emotional and memory centers (in the limbic system).

Dr. Mayberg found that Area 25 runs hyperactive or "hot" in depressed and sad people, acting like a gate left open that allows negative emotions to overwhelm rational thinking and mood. It appears that Area 25 works overtime as it either tries to temper a depressive loop set up between the emotional and thinking centers or actually causes the problem by kicking into overdrive and letting depressive loops take over (Mayberg 1997; Dobbs 2006). Inserting electrodes into that area of the brain to close the gate rapidly alleviated depression in two-thirds of the very deeply depressed people in her study (Mayberg et al. 2005; Dobbs 2006).

In further research on Area 25, it was found that when feelings of sadness passed, Area 25 calmed. In fact, Area 25 was overly busy in all types of depression and was calmed by any successful therapy. Whenever drugs, placebos, or psychotherapy worked to release depression, even temporarily, there was also a calming in Area 25. When cognitive behavioral therapy (CBT) helped people recognize and change or release thought patterns that would otherwise depress them, Area 25 calmed. Brain scans showed a tug of war between the depressive thoughts and moods and the patients' attempts to think their way out of those moods and to self-correct. When those attempts were successful, Area 25 could relax (Goldapple et al. 2004; Dobbs 2006).

The current theory is that Area 25 is part of a neural and hormonal survival system to respond to acute threats, but this system turns corrosive when stress memories and persistent negative thoughts trigger the survival system continuously. Mood disorders develop when extreme or continuous stress kicks the limbic system's fear and anxiety centers into long-term overdrive. Area 25 is like a switch in the circuit. If you can trip the circuit out of survival mode, then the body and brain can settle back to normal.

This research on Area 25 confirms an emerging network model of the brain and mood. Reason and passion, thought and emotion, are linked in a circuit. Rather than one dominating the other, they engage in a conversation that either reinforces the other or changes the other.

The Cut-Thru technique (provided in the next chapter) is designed to be a circuit breaker, transforming the dialogue between thoughts and emotions to bring you breakthrough perceptions and insights. Then the Cut-Thru technique engages the automatic feedback loop between emotion and thought to work in your *favor* and provide you with new power for transforming depression.

With the Cut-Thru technique, as you trip the switch by self-generating a positive emotion, even just a little, and increase heart rhythm coherence, you begin to perceive differently. As you sustain coherence and release overidentification through practicing the steps, new perceptions and feelings take hold and you *reverse the polarity* of the feedback loop. You start an upward-spiraling momentum out of the funk, leading to appreciable increases in well-being.

The capacity to self-generate a positive emotion remains a largely untapped human power, but that's only because people haven't developed it. Positive psychology researchers theorize that positive emotions loosen the tourniquet that negative emotions exert on the mind and heart by dismantling the narrowed perspectives and unbalanced biochemical reactions caused by negative conscious or subconscious emotional undercurrents (Fredrickson 2000, 2001). Intentionally generating a positive emotion creates different neural traffic and communication between the heart and brain (McCraty et al. 2006), broadening your habitual mode of thinking, building resilience, and delivering that highly sought-after quality—contentment (Fredrickson 2000).

Contentment is a physiological state that expands people's self-view and worldview. Research at the Institute of HeartMath has found that returning a person's heart rhythms to more coherent functioning powers up positive emotions to create the physiological changes needed for perceiving a wider array of possibilities. Positive emotion opens the intuitive connection with your heart—your *core self*—and invites your real spirit in.

To power up positive emotion, especially when you haven't felt much of it due to long-term depression, it's important to understand the *feeling world of depression*.

Understanding a Funk

When they describe the feeling of depression, many people say they're "in a *funk*." So many people feel funky or dulled-out a lot but don't know why because nothing seems to be wrong. When you feel the funk inside, you can't always trace it back to its source. You question what happened. To make matters worse, the funky feeling can come and go, and you wonder why.

Trevor had this experience:

I was at a party wondering how my spirits got so low, when I had been excited about going to this party. I kept thinking this should be fun because I like everyone, as the cloud of funk settled in. I felt I should feel happier. I had had high sales at work that week, my physical exam showed I was in the best of health, and my kid had made the soccer team. But I didn't feel up to my usual self. What's most baffling was, this cloud of funk descended on me many days for no obvious reason. I also had great days when it didn't. I never knew which kind of day it would be.

Funky feelings occur when there is incomplete communication on one side or another of a two-way communication circuit, whether it's between your mind and heart or between you and another person. If the funk doesn't clear, it starts to accumulate, creating an internal sensation of darkness or density in your system. People describe the sensation differently: a sensation of cobwebs in the brain or something that reminds them of grimy contacts on a battery or a sensation in the heart area that's like Velcro or cement or as chains around the heart.

A major problem with accumulated funk that has piled up over time is that the mood gets stored in the unconscious and exerts its influence randomly when you least expect it and least want it. Funk stored in the unconscious can ride around inside, popping to the surface sometimes as mental funk, sometimes as emotional, sometimes as physical aches and pains. Strong funky feelings can consume your thoughts and attention in self-absorption as you try to do something to free yourself.

Release Blame

Practicing the Cut-Thru technique will give you more capacity to release and blow out the funk. One of the most important things to release is fault-finding or blame toward yourself or another. Blame keeps your spirit in retreat. To bring in more of your spirit, you need to take full responsibility for your own energies, regardless of what someone else has done. You have to realize that you do have the heart power to release judgment, resentment, or hostility. You do it for your own health and well-being if for no other reason.

The coherent energy from Cut-Thru practice will reconnect you with deeper heart feelings. It will bring in more of your spirit to help lift your perspective on issues that have bothered you for a long time so that, step-by-step, you can free yourself from the rest of the funk.

Heart Lock-In and Cut-Thru are *emotion restructuring techniques.* As you practice them, you restructure your emotional habits and rewire your circuitry. That's why regular and consistent practice of both techniques is important. We suggest practicing them five times per week. You can practice more often of course, but set a regular program and stick with it for a month. That's not a long time considering how much more time you've invested in depression loops. Use the other tools you've learned—Notice and Ease, Power of Neutral, Quick Coherence, and Attitude Breathing—to clear as you go throughout the day. Commitment to a practice plan is an investment in your empowerment.

Bringing in heart intelligence involves increasing the ratio of time you spend in your heart (at peace and in a positive flow) as compared to out of your heart (in your head and emotional reactions).

Without heart intelligence, your untamed mind and emotions will keep you duped into believing that your vitality is being squandered by external circumstances beyond your control. It's from heart intelligence that you gain the insights and heart intent to make the attitudinal changes you need to take emotional responsibility.

Out the Pout

Take the "big deal" out of whatever comes up as you practice and take the significance, self-pity, and pout out of whatever cards you've been dealt in life. The answers to many unsolved mysteries of your life are to be found right underneath your depression. The more regularly you adhere to a structured practice program, the more power you will accumulate to clear out cellular residue. You are not going to be able to "out all pout" overnight. But you will gain a lot of free energy seeing how fast Cut-Thru can work. This gives you more commitment to keep going.

You can gauge the degree of heart power you're building by observing the distance between "hear" and "do." That's the time between when you hear your heart intelligence and when you *act* on it. Transmuting the funk that's stored in the cells changes the vibratory rhythm of your cellular structure, bringing it into sync with your deeper heart, empowering you to more quickly put into practice what your heart intelligence says. Do that and you will find more happiness.

Learn to ask your heart to help you as you practice. Talk to your heart like a close buddy—a buddy you can be vulnerable with, who doesn't judge and can't wait to help. Be sincere and open to inner guidance.

Be on the lookout for a "cellular pout." Pouting is deeper than whining about any one thing. It's like the tantrums little children throw when they don't get what they want. If you've had extended occasions of falling into self-pity or throwing inner tantrums when life didn't go your way, this can imprint an underlying pout into your cellular memory. You may think you've let go of your self-pity, but your cells can retain a childish pout long after you think you're done with it. This can lead to strong emotional mood swings, at times either too ebullient or too pitiful.

Unconscious, cumulative cellular pout is one of the chief contributors to ongoing depression. A pout can seem innocent. Why not complain and pout inside? Everybody does. And who would know? But pout accumulates until it casts a pall on your worldview. Even when you *know* you are pouting and want to stop, the weight of accumulation can make it hard to do anything about it. Then you start pouting about that, and this makes it even worse.

Some people take on feeling pitiful as part of their identity. Cellular pout runs a subtle but continuous energy drain in their bodies, affecting them at the hormonal level. If you want to feel better permanently, then you have to address how you spend your energy. You have to learn how to out the pout!

Cut-Thru practice will reveal the looping patterns that have trapped you in pout. It will guide you to the heart vulnerability—the opening of your heart—needed to bring in more spirit for emotional healing. This exposes and releases the trapped judgments and the unseen overidentities and overcares. Life can still seem tough, but it can be tougher if you don't cut through.

When self-pity and pout are your problem, spend time with Cut-Thru step 1 (see chapter 9) to become more aware of how you feel inside about anything. Practice Notice and Ease and become heart vulnerable to yourself without sinking into self-pity. Don't worry if you feel like you're trying to pry open a clam. Just keep practicing, and your heart intelligence will help you.

Spend time with Cut-Thru step 2, breathing core heart feelings like love, appreciation, care, or compassion through the heart and solar plexus to bring your heart rhythms into greater coherence. Then radiate that coherence to your cells.

When you're finished with your Cut-Thru practice session, move on with what's next in your life even if there is some residual funky feeling or pout. Assign what's left to soak in the heart and move on. As you keep doing this, you *will* free your cells from the pout.

Another thing to watch out for while clearing out cellular pout is a quiet or loud feeling of "It's not fair." Memories of what's not been fair are one of the major components of pout, and they will come to the surface to be cleared out. Don't get caught in their net.

It's only human for people to use their view of what was fair or unfair as a way to substantiate what they think they know. In most cases, they're substantiating a hurt ego and are not open to another perspective. They've set themselves up as judge and jury, decided that what happened was not right or fair, and sentenced *themselves* to prison without realizing it. Whether you feel that others, God, or life treated you unfairly, the effect on you is the same. While thinking that you are blaming something outside yourself, you are putting your heart, mind, and cells on the receiving end of the sentence.

So if you are going to regain your freedom and happiness, you have to release feelings of "it's unfair" or "my situation is so different" that underlie the pout. What you need is to reach a new state of neutral so that you can unlock the prison door. In many situations, you will never achieve the larger understanding you crave until you can really go to neutral. In neutral, you can ask yourself, "What if there is another picture or another purpose to this than what I'm seeing?" and be open to receiving new information.

When your feelings are screaming or whispering "It's not fair!" spend more time with Cut-Thru step 3. Assume objectivity as if it were someone else's problem so that you can find a real neutral. Increase compassion to depersonalize the issue, so it's not all about you. See it from a larger perspective. As you take out overidentity, you'll see old things with new eyes.

Laura's story describes why letting go of "fair or unfair" comparisons was so important in lifting her depression.

> *I'd experienced a lot of depression as a young woman but had learned ways to keep the black hole at bay. That bleak, unyielding feeling state had gradually become a thing of the past for me. I had almost forgotten what it felt like. Then, at age forty-eight, my partner of many years surprised me with the news that he was leaving me and relocating across the country. He said it wasn't personal, but he needed a change and had to go.*

Laura was devastated. They had lived very modestly, and now she faced not only the loss of the relationship, but severely diminished finances as well. "It may not have seemed personal to him," Laura said, "but it felt very personal to me! I felt a powerful sense of injustice at the loss and felt blame and anger at being left broke. I was middle-aged and single on top of it all. It wasn't fair, pure and simple. I had been lampooned by life, or that's how it seemed. I felt I was a good person who clearly didn't deserve this kind of treatment from life."

After her partner left, Laura had to move out of the home they had been leasing. She took a room in the home of a family she knew, which placed her within walking distance to work.

> *At first, the emotional shock of the change kept me busy adjusting to the new lifestyle, but after a while, I realized I was depressed and it was getting worse. It's hard to describe, but my depression felt like a seeping drip that rots the area around the leak but isn't noticed until you open the cupboard under the dripping faucet to look for something long forgotten.*

About this time Laura learned Cut-Thru and found that it helped shift her out of depression into peace and into deeper compassion—for herself and others.

> *To do this has been enormously empowering. I turned the steps into action steps and attitudes to hold throughout the day. This is what worked for me:*
>
> Sincerity in Appreciating—*I made it a habit to be aware of a negative feeling state and to stop and ask myself, "What do I appreciate, in this moment, right now?" There was always something to appreciate when I asked my heart, and often I was surprised to see what it was. Diligence with this step not only while I did my Cut-Thru practice but during the day made a serious dent in releasing my depression and getting me to a new state of neutral.*

Take the Significance Out or Dissolve the Significance—*I've come to love this step when I'm feeling anxiety or resistance. I can feel the release if I just keep at it. And it's common sense. I know this is how I would help a friend try to see the situation if it was her life.*

Be in the Now—*This attitude helped me stop lamenting about what I'd lost and stop the dread and blind alleys my fear projections showed me as my future, colored as they were by depression. When I'd wake myself up and "'Be in the Now," in this moment, everything would shift and be all right. Then I'd find myself automatically circling around to appreciation again.*

It may sound simplistic, but for anyone who's experienced depression, to know there is freedom from that state by incorporating simple techniques and tools into daily life is a miracle. It's a miracle that can help us "walking wounded" become healthy and whole again and able to go on to develop our full potential with a peaceful heart and with care to give the world around us.

Create a Cut-Thru Practice Program

Creating a Cut-Thru practice program will provide the quickest results for lifting long-term depression. Study and practice the six steps of the Cut-Thru technique given in the next chapter. Ask your heart to help you address the accumulated funk at the cellular level.

Your cells can put up resistance for a while. You can feel like part of you is fighting against your heart intent. That's because your circuits have been wired into a depression loop, which can create resistance as you make efforts to change. Remember: *that wiring isn't you.* You'll start to see this more objectively as you practice.

You'll see that resistance comes from old cellular feelings and perceptions flowing along old wiring. The cellular world often seems to have a mind of its own, which is why a funk can seem so potent or create a fear that you'll be "nothing" without all the stored hurt, blame, and pouting. Just stay committed to using the tools. Your heart knows what needs to be addressed.

In the next chapter, you will learn about setting up a practice program to help you release depression feedback loops once and for all.

chapter 9

Creating a Cut-Thru Practice Program

We're all familiar with the expression to "cut through." It means to "get to the heart of the matter." To release depression feedback loops and funk, you don't need to sort through all the details of your past. You simply address the perceptions, feelings, and thoughts that come up while you're using the technique.

Cut-Thru's six short steps take you through the process. Each time you repeat them, old perceptions and feelings will rise to the surface to be released from your cells. As you build more heart intelligence and coherence with Cut-Thru, you will transform depression into insight and effective action. You'll be able to release your stored emotional investment in long-standing issues and grievances and free yourself.

Approaching Cut-Thru practice with a heart-focused "I mean business" attitude accelerates clearing. After you go through the steps a few times, it will get simpler. Read through the explanations of the steps to understand how the process unfolds. The wording of each step is designed to help you build, in stages, the coherence you will need to release the deeper issues.

Practicing Heart Lock-In first—sending positive feelings and attitudes to yourself, to people or issues—even for five minutes before you practice the Cut-Thru steps, will increase your capacity to sustain coherence as you go through the Cut-Thru steps. When you make genuine efforts to approach Cut-Thru from a more coherent, peaceful state, more of your real spirit can come in to help.

To get started, pick an issue. Don't pick your most loaded or most stressful issue to start. Pick a minor issue to learn on, even though it may bring up a deeper issue as you use Cut-Thru.

Create a Cut-Thru worksheet on a piece of paper or in your journal or notebook. (See the directions for making a work-sheet on the last two pages of this chapter.) Read each step and the explanation. Then practice the step on your issue, and write your response on the Cut-Thru worksheet. Do the same with all the steps.

When you have finished, look back and read your responses to each step to gain more understanding. Listen to what your heart intelligence tells you, as you go. If you are uncertain about anything, go through the steps again to get more clarity.

The Cut-Thru Technique

Step 1. Be aware of how you feel about the issue at hand.

Step 2. Center yourself by breathing in through the heart and out through the solar plexus. Breathe love and appreciation through this area for thirty seconds or longer to help anchor your attention there.

Step 3. Assume objectivity about the feeling or issue—as if it were someone else's problem.

Step 4. Rest in neutral—in your rational, mature heart.

Step 5. Soak and relax any disturbed or perplexing feelings in the compassion of the heart. Dissolve the significance a little at a time. Remember it's not the problem that causes energy drain as much as the stored significance that you have assigned to the problem.

Step 6. After dissolving as much significance as you can, from your deep heart sincerely ask for appropriate guidance or insight. If you don't get an answer, find something to appreciate for a while.

Practicing Cut-Thru

Now it's your turn to practice the steps. Find a place where you can practice Cut-Thru without interruptions or distractions from people, telephones, pets, or anything else for ten to fifteen minutes (or less, if you arrive at your objective sooner). Approach practice sessions with a genuine attitude instead of trying to find a quick fix to get the monkey off your back.

Each time you go through the Cut-Thru steps, it can help to release some of your overidentity or overcare, and that will begin to release some of the funk. At the beginning, you may feel like you did when you first learned to use a computer—hunting and pecking at the keys, not sure which command to use next. With some practice, you'll be gaining access to your intuitive heart intelligence as easily as you now turn on your computer each morning.

Step 1: Be Aware of How You Feel

Be aware of how you feel about the issue at hand. Be honest with yourself. Just as you learned in using the Notice and Ease tool, admitting how you feel is the first step in release. Most people notice thoughts constantly flitting through their minds. It's harder to notice feelings skimming under the surface. This is because emotions occur faster than thoughts and faster than your mind's ability to intercept them.

Many times, how you feel will be clear and easy to name: angry, anxious, overwhelmed, blocked, guilty, sad, happy, loving, and so forth. Other times, there may be confusing undercurrents of feelings. Just name whatever feelings you can.

On some issues you may have "numbed out" your feelings. Perhaps it's because you don't want to feel bad or because you have too much past hurt to want to stay in touch with your feelings. The problem, as you have learned in previous chapters, is that even if you try to ignore disturbed feelings or pretend they're not there, your subconscious emotional undercurrents stay absorbed in them. You can shove them aside, but they are still depleting your energy. So the first step of Cut-Thru—being aware of how you feel—is critical to the process of transforming depression.

Write down your issue and how you feel about it on your Cut-Thru worksheet.

Step 2: Breathe a Positive Feeling or Attitude

Center yourself by breathing in through the heart and out through the solar plexus. Breathe love and appreciation through this area for thirty seconds or longer to help anchor your attention there.

Breathing in through the area of the heart and out through the solar plexus (located about four inches below the heart, just below the sternum) helps keep your emotional energies anchored or grounded. The solar plexus area, like the heart, has its own little brain with neurons, neurotransmitters, and oscillating rhythms (Gershon 1999).

When you experience a frightening situation, your brain tells the adrenal glands to release stress hormones that prepare the body to fight or flee. Your stomach contains many sensory nerves that are stimulated by these stress hormones. That's why you feel sensations of anxiety or fear in the solar plexus area or get a knot in your stomach when you're upset.

Many people confuse "gut feelings" with their heart, but, in fact, the gut brain is more instinctive than intuitive. It's your heart that provides sensitive intuition that brings understanding. When the gut brain synchronizes with the heart, you have more clarity and power.

Step 2 brings the gut brain into synchronization with the heart. Breathing a positive feeling or attitude, like love or appreciation—in through the heart and out through the solar plexus—helps generate the coherent power needed to release resistant feelings.

Imagine breathing the positive feeling or attitude in through your heart and exhaling out through your solar plexus to help anchor the positive attitude. Don't stress about whether you are doing it right. Just practice this gently and sincerely. After thirty seconds or so, you may find your emotions shifting toward an easier state. Strong emotional reactions will need longer, especially if your issue is about a deep hurt or wounded vanity. Be genuine and stay with it.

If you have the time, practice step 2 for several minutes. Just like with the Attitude Breathing tool, if you can't find a feeling of love or appreciation, breathe the attitude of appreciation for something—anything—to get more in sync. It's worth the effort.

Write on your Cut-Thru worksheet what you feel and perceive from practicing step 2.

Step 3: Assume Objectivity

Assume objectivity about the feeling or issue—as if it were someone else's problem. Step 3 involves finding the maturity to disengage from an issue for a few moments in order to let the emotions release and come back to balance. You can pretend you are watching another person dealing with your issue. It's like looking at yourself from a distance or from the point of view of your higher self. This helps give you a more dispassionate and objective view.

You might imagine yourself as another person sitting a few feet away or standing below you, as if you are watching this person from a helicopter or from a bird's-eye view. One of the first things you may notice is how much more compassionate and understanding you are toward this other person than you have been toward yourself. Compassion is a core heart feeling that also helps increase heart rhythm coherence and synchronization between the heart and brain.

Most of the time, when your emotions get hung up on an issue, it's because you are overidentified or overattached. You need to learn how to step back from the issue and say, "I'm not the same as this problem" so that you can keep a more open mind about what is really happening.

Marriage counselors and mediators spend about 80 percent of their time trying to get their clients to step back and see things more objectively. The same is needed when mediating a dispute within yourself. You'll never get anywhere if your mind is made up and your emotions are rigid.

Whatever you perceive in step 3, keep your attention and energy focused in the heart to stay in coherence. As an emotion or issue releases, you might feel it all over again—old perceptions, thoughts, and feelings spinning out from cellular storage. That's part of the process. Befriend but don't buy into those feelings all over again. Remain objective about whatever your feelings are doing. It can seem you're going backward, but you're not. It helps to remind yourself that it's just stored attitudes of blame, anxiety, sadness, hopelessness, or pout that are spinning out.

If the emotions still overtake you, it's okay. Don't fight them. Just go back to step 2 and breathe and radiate genuine care or compassion for yourself to regain your composure. Know that your root motive to care about the issue is right but that you're getting caught up again in the emotions surrounding the issue. Knowing this is caring for yourself. Have compassion for yourself—it's only human, but you don't have to stay there. You can cut through.

Step 3 helps you to step outside the emotions so that you can get to a more neutral place. When you get to neutral, your heart intelligence can intuitively guide this "other person"—you—to new perceptions.

Write down any shifts in perception or glimpses at a new way to look at and address the issue after practicing step 3 on your Cut-Thru worksheet.

Step 4: Rest in Neutral

Rest in neutral in your rational, mature heart. By finding some objectivity, you get closer to a state of neutral and can rest in a more peaceful heart. Steps 1 through 3 help you become more neutral about issues that have strong negative emotional accumulation or stacked stress. Being neutral doesn't mean that you have to agree with anything that happened. It simply means becoming neutral toward uncomfortable feelings, thoughts, and memories about the issue. This gives you more empowerment and reduces their energy drain.

Try to relax and ease feelings and thoughts that are not neutral into the heart, just as you do when using the Notice and Ease and the Power of Neutral tools. This allows the heart to realign incoherent emotional energy. It provides an opportunity for more peace and new possibilities to emerge. In some situations you may be assuming you know someone's motives when you don't really know. In neutral, you ask yourself, "What if there's something I don't know?" The attitude of "I don't really know" helps the mind become humble and open so that heart intelligence can surface to show you a new perspective. Even if what happened was tough and you were hurt or traumatized, in neutral you can still ask yourself, "Haven't I drained enough from this? Isn't it time to at least try to neutralize the stored energies, to get on with my life?"

The *rational, mature heart* is a place inside that is sober and balanced in its attitudes. The balance provided by heart intelligence will allow your intuition to present you with commonsense go-forward strategies that are best for you and everyone involved.

Practice step 4, and then write down your feelings and perceptions on your Cut-Thru worksheet. If you find that you were not able to remain neutral, don't worry. This is normal at first, especially if the issue has a lot of hurt or sadness and emotional investment associated with it. You aren't bad. You aren't failing. Just go back to step 2 for a few moments, breathing compassion for yourself—in through your heart and out through your solar plexus—so you become more grounded. Then move through steps 3 and 4 again until you can rest in a more neutral, mature heart that is willing to say, "What if I wasn't bad?" or "What if I really don't have the whole picture?" or "It's time to forgive myself (or another) and move on" and mean it.

Steps 1 through 4 have prepared you for the last steps of the technique, which will help you to dismantle depression feedback loops at neural-electrical and biochemical levels. As you practice steps 5 and 6 over time, you clear out residues and lay in a new pattern.

Step 5: Soak and Relax

Soak and relax any disturbed or perplexing feelings in the compassion of the heart. Dissolve the significance a little at a time. When you feel disturbed about something, remember it's not the issue itself that's causing you discomfort. It's the importance or emotional significance that you have invested in the issue.

In step 5, you ease perplexing feelings and memories back to the heart and soak them there to dissolve the significance. Keep relaxing resistances (funky feelings, compressed or stuck energy) you may be feeling in the heart. Just allow resistance or heaviness to simply soak in the energy of the heart. Don't worry if it doesn't release entirely. Feeling compassion for yourself will accelerate the process.

On major issues, it's nearly impossible not to have assigned a lot of significance. And that's all right. But now it's time to start anew. Knowing that stored significance will only keep creating funk and draining your energy, you can commit now—more than ever—to releasing it.

In step 5, you use the coherent power of the heart to end this chapter in your life. Have respect for yourself and compassion for having gone through that experience. After all, you were hurt. Now it's time to release any self-judgments or feelings of having "done bad" in response to the situation. It's all okay. You can take out a lot of the significance by knowing that many others would have reacted in the same way. This helps you to more quickly forgive and release the issue within your system. Often your heart will suggest you talk to a person, and you'll need to have that heart-vulnerable conversation before the stuck feelings release.

Through steady practice of step 5, you can align yourself with a new commitment and heart intent to move forward. What is important to your healing is your ability to keep your heart open and release the entrapments your mind insists should have happened instead. Soak any feeling of "poor me" out of your system. Being a victim doesn't serve you. It only keeps the same old feelings spinning round and round. You've already done this enough.

Take your time with this step. Emotional histories and long-term depression become deeply ingrained patterns in your neural cells, which is why they keep resurfacing and taking hold of you. Depending on how deep these feelings go and how much reinforcement they've had, there may be a lot of emotional energy stored in them. Dissolving and taking out significance is probably *the most important part* of the Cut-Thru technique. As you dissolve the significance and transform the stored incoherent energy, you change the circuitry and release the pattern, resulting in more peace and satisfaction.

Practice step 5, then write down your feelings and perceptions on your Cut-Thru worksheet. Assign unresolved feelings to soak and dissolve in the heart as you move on to step 6.

Step 6: Ask for Guidance; Appreciate

After dissolving as much significance as you can, sincerely ask, from your deep heart, for appropriate guidance or insight. Now, after having done steps 1 through 5, you are more able to hear your heart intelligence. The heart doesn't always flash its answer on a neon sign. A lot of times, heart intelligence comes to you softly and subtly. When people talk about the "still, small voice" of the heart, they are saying that the heart communicates through a delicate intuitive feeling or subtle knowing. It's important to follow even fleeting heart perceptions. If a perception is peaceful and feels good to you, that's your signal to follow it, even if it seems too simple or easy.

Now practice step 6, and write your feelings and perceptions on your Cut-Thru worksheet. Don't despair if you don't get an "aha" insight on the spot. Sometimes you will draw a blank. That can be an indicator that the most helpful approach for now is to put the issue aside for a while and move on.

The most effective way to move on is to find something to appreciate. Take whatever glimmers of peace or release you have gained from Cut-Thru and appreciate them, or just choose something in life to appreciate to help keep you from being pulled back as deeply into the old patterns. Intentionally generating appreciation often brings clarity on other issues you are working on, so it's a productive use of your time and energy.

Close your Cut-Thru session by doing Attitude Breathing for thirty seconds or longer, breathing appreciation to help you rise above the issue you've been cutting through and move on to something else. Allow insights to come to you later as you put your attention elsewhere.

Take Action

Remember to keep writing down any glimmers of new perceptions so you can remember them. If you don't act on your insights, they can fade or you can begin to doubt them, especially when they involve a need to communicate honestly and sincerely with someone. Take the power of your heart intent and have the courage to put your insights into action. Watch how things can improve.

After Kelly practiced Cut-Thru a few times on her issues with her husband, who had left her several years before for another woman, she told us that steps 5 and 6 were her keys to a new life.

> As I was dissolving the significance, I realized that I have
> blamed my ex so much for everything—for controlling my life,
> for our lower standard of living, for having betrayed not only

me, but our son. If he did that to us, then I must have been a
failure as a wife and person. That's my depression loop.
If I take the significance out of all this, then I'm really okay.
None of this is really me. I've hurt myself with all the blame.
By dissolving the significance, I can stop hurting myself.
I know I'll have to keep practicing the Cut-Thru, because
I've been churning around in that depression loop for so
long that it's sometimes automatic, waking me up in my
sleep. But I have a glimmer of hope of how I will be without it.
The real me. I can appreciate that.

You may be surprised at the warmhearted intelligence or
new insights you gain from Cut-Thru in only a few sittings.
Even if you slide back and the old perceptions and feeling
loops take over, just keep practicing.

For a time period, old mental and emotional patterns will
try to get in the way of moving the depression out of your
system. They can act like the tail of a dragon. You've had new
inspiration and released some of the depression, but as you
turn the corner to feeling better, the dragon's tail of the pattern
snaps back and whips you. Here's what might happen and
what to do.

Beware of whining. Your heart gives you clarity on which
way to go, and you start out with the best intentions, but then
there's a part of you that decides to whine or moan and groan
about having to do that. Sometimes that part can feel like an
emotional or stubborn child inside.

If you find yourself beginning to whine, spend extra time
with step 3, rest in neutral, in your rational, mature heart,
and apply "business heart." Tell yourself, "I can't afford this
anymore," then keep easing the whining thoughts and feelings
out through your heart.

Recall all the energy that you already have spent going
round and round chasing your tail on the same old thing.

Breathe through the heart and solar plexus to anchor the attitude of "I mean business" in your cells. If the whine comes back, keep going back to your rational, mature heart, telling yourself, "Enough—I don't need this anymore. I absolutely cannot afford it."

Long-standing accumulated identities or self-worth issues (for example, feeling like a failure) take time to completely unravel, and each person's spirit works with them in a different way. Just keep going for it. With sincere practice, you'll reach a place where some of the problems you've been working on and working out for a long time begin to finally come to resolution.

✐ Setting Up a Practice Program

Make a list of issues you'd like to use Cut-Thru on to gain more heart intelligence. Include habitual reactions and moods you'd like to cut through. If you can't associate a mood with a particular issue, just use the mood or feeling as the issue at hand, and go through the steps to gain more insight.

Practice the Cut-Thru steps in ten-minute sessions (longer if you like), five times a week. To make your practice simpler, you can record the steps at a pace that feels right to you. Then you can listen to the recording and guide yourself through the steps without getting distracted by reading them. Have a pencil and a Cut-Thru worksheet in front of you, and pause the recording to write down your feelings and perceptions after each step.

Use the Heart Lock-In technique five times a week to help increase coherence and sustain the insights you will be building with Cut-Thru. If you have difficulty with any of the Cut-Thru steps, experiment with the order of the steps. Some people find it beneficial to first do steps 1 and 2 to increase coherence, then go to steps 5 and 6 to dissolve significance in order to let go of resistance and achieve a more objective, neutral understanding in steps 3 and 4.

After your first few sessions of committed practice to the Cut-Thru technique, you'll start to find the rhythm of how the six steps energetically flow. Once you find the flow, you will be able to move through them in shorter time periods. Eventually you'll be able to just use one or more of the Quick Cut-Thru steps below to find release.

Quick Cut-Thru Steps

Step 1. Be Aware of How You Feel

Step 2. Breathe a Positive Feeling or Attitude

Step 3. Assume Objectivity

Step 4. Rest in Neutral

Step 5. Soak and Relax

Step 6. Ask for Guidance; Appreciate

Cut-Thru Worksheet

Divide a piece of paper into six sections—one section for each step. Write down the heading or questions for each section as given in the box below and leave enough room between headings to write your answers. This is your Cut-Thru worksheet. Make copies to use in the future.

Write the date of each session to keep track of your progress and remind you of what your heart intelligence is showing you.

Be sure to practice Cut-Thru on one issue at a time. If you can't formulate an issue, use sadness, fear, or whatever you are feeling as your issue. If more issues pop up as you go through the steps, don't worry—that's part of the clearing process. Just keep going through the steps and following your heart. If a particular concern keeps popping up, do another Cut-Thru session just on that issue.

Six Sections of Your Cut-Thru Worksheet

Step 1. What is my issue?

Step 2. Describe any shifts in feeling or perceptions after practicing step 2.

Step 3. What would I tell another person with this issue? Describe any subtle or obvious shift in perceptions after practicing step 3.

Step 4. What options do I see from a more neutral state? Describe any feeling or perception shifts from practicing step 4.

Step 5. On a scale of 1 to 10, how much significance have I invested in this issue? Describe any feeling or perception shifts after practicing step 5.

Step 6. Cut-Thru response: what feeling or insight is my heart intelligence offering me?

chapter 10

Resolving Relationship Conflicts

Depression is often helped, or even cured, by clearing unresolved relationship conflicts out of your system. Psychological
gridlocks develop when you strongly imprint hurt, betrayal,
or strong emotional pain in your neurons and cells. Often the
gridlock stems from self-worth issues, guilt, or self-blame. The
stored energy from unresolved, high-impact conflicts with
others or conflicts within yourself shuts you off from your heart.
This creates blockages that interrupt the natural energy flow of
spirit through your mental, emotional, and biological systems.
When you are not connected to your deeper heart, your spirit's
interactive flow within yourself is progressively stifled.

People have different natures that are vulnerable to different emotional tendencies. For example, when someone has
a very caring nature, they also tend to fall into overcaring
and worry. This can cause them to jam up inside and repress
their feelings. For others, it's easier to succumb to a downward
negative emotional spiral when others around them are down.
For people, men especially, who are goal driven and tend to

push aside feelings, there can be a strong tendency toward frustration and anger.

It's important to respect that people have different personality tendencies and awareness gaps. Through Cut-Thru practice, your heart intelligence will start to open you to a wider bandwidth of perception. This gives you the capability to see and correct your gaps and resolve relationship conflicts. Everyone has perception gaps, and learning to widen your perception is a process of growth. Depending on their natures, people move slowly or quickly in different aspects of growth. Through the heart, people come to understand this and learn to help each other, no matter what their natures.

Greg, a financial planner, told us this story:

To say I was depressed is an understatement. I did not sleep well for months. I'd lost a lot of money in speculation and thought I would have to sell the house. I was terrified my wife would leave me if she knew. My heart knew what I had to do, but I wouldn't do it. I had to come clean, but I was so afraid of the outcome I could not act, even though my heart and conscience knew what was right.

Just because you know what the right thing is, it doesn't stop you from doing the wrong thing and avoiding doing the right thing. It takes power to listen to your heart and act on what you know. That's the power that the HeartMath tools gave me.

My HeartMath coach gave me tools to listen to my heart and to speak my truth in spite of fear. When I finally came clean with my wife and my business partners, the release of energy from relief afforded me tremendous opportunities I never could have seen in my depression. It's not that they were pleased or even kind about it, once I told them what I'd done, but I was back in integrity with myself.

Cut-Thru gave me a tremendous amount of power to heal those relationships I had betrayed as well as to innovate solutions that have put my family, my business, and me in better positions than ever before. Now I am measuring success not just by financial statements, but by the quality of emotion and vitality I have within myself and get to share with others. I am happier than ever before.

Before HeartMath, I had convinced myself that getting rich would solve my stress. "If only we had more money," I kept telling myself. Now I realize that money does not solve things, but attitude does. As long as I was trying to solve things with money, I was putting the power outside of me. I was still trying to do it with something external—not from my heart.

HeartMath gave me back the reins, and now I don't go up and down with my financial gains and drains. I am so grateful for the power of the heart, and the power of the HeartMath tools to access it.

Using Your Heart Power in Communication

Most people who tend to depression have a hard time expressing their feelings to those closest to them. HeartMath gives you tools and techniques to shift polarity from head to heart and move toward authentic communication. Emotional stuff will always go on between people. That's the nature of life. But emotional responsibility means using your heart power to clear up current and old relationship issues.

Depressed people often avoid communication for fear it will turn into conflict. You can override this tendency by listening to the promptings of your heart when it says to talk to someone. Use your heart power to follow your heart.

Precede your conversation with someone else with a Heart Lock-In, sending care and compassion. Speak the truth of your feelings from your heart while you continue to send the energy of care or compassion. Listen genuinely from your heart with a quiet mind, without thinking about how you will respond.

Use Attitude Breathing to stay centered if you start to react. As you practice this authentic communication, you'll see how in the past you've compromised your integrity or tried to overplease people (which doesn't please anyone) based on fear projections of how they'll respond.

Practice putting out the energy of care, both in a Heart Lock-In and as you go about your day, whether you have communication problems or not. This preventive maintenance helps you have more latitude for someone else's nature, yet not let them roll over you.

Remember, authentic heart communication is not an invitation to be used as a doormat. Speak sincerely from the heart, but draw the line if you need to, and express firmness or an "I mean business" attitude at the same time. It takes courage and practice to master this combination, but it's well worth the effort to find your own empowerment. It won't happen all at once, but you can learn to put on a solid business heart and say what your heart tells you to say without worrying about being walked over.

All the things people *don't* communicate in relationships make up the biggest obstacle to heart-based relating. After talking a while, one person may say, "I'm all right; are you all right?" They agree they're fine, but one or both go off and seethe.

Much of the time resentments continue because of over-caring about not having spoken to another person from your heart. You may have unloaded, or you may have wimped out and said nothing because you didn't want to make waves. Or you may have excused yourself with, "Well, I have faults too, so I shouldn't say anything." All of this blocks heart communication and conflict resolution.

Learn to practice being heart vulnerable and honest about your feelings in communications, and face off your fears. Heart vulnerability means speaking and listening from the heart as sincerely as you can. When you communicate, people may not remember exactly what you said, but they remember *how you made them feel.*

You can drain yourself emotionally and physically by investing so much in wanting to be understood. Worrying about how you'll come off during an interaction is a head focus and stops your sincere heart. You end up rehearsing what to say, or replaying and rehashing what you wished you'd said and churning "All I meant was ..." over and over. Often that "need to be understood" is masking a deeper "need to be right" or to control.

Phyllis discovered this in her Cut-Thru practice.

In my relationship with my boyfriend, John, I kept feeling frustrated because as soon as we'd start arguing a little bit, he'd no longer listen to me. I can't tell you how many arguments we have had late into the night with me repeating, "What I'm trying to say is ..." all to no avail. He'd never "get" what I was telling him. He'd just turn into this brick wall.

The pattern of their arguments wearied them both. The life was draining out of their relationship, and after months of these disagreements, Phyllis was feeling deeply hurt and misunderstood. Through practicing Cut-Thru she saw how she was contributing to the trouble.

I looked deeper at my need to be understood and saw that what I really wanted was to teach John something. I thought I was seeing how things really [were] and wanting John to

*agree with me. I practiced being neutral when we'd talk
and immediately began to notice a deep, insistent feeling
that he get what I was trying to say. I let go of the need
to be understood—which was really the need to teach him
something. As soon as I stopped, it seemed to free John.
He no longer put up that brick wall. We started talking
and stopped fighting.*

You'll start to see your motives as you practice Cut-Thru. If you take the attitude of wanting to see, from a neutral place, your part in a relationship dynamic, then your heart intuition can come in and show you a truer picture of what is going on or what to say next. Neutral in the heart is a place that opens a door to new insight. Often the heart's insight is to just let it go for now. New understandings or the appropriate things to say will come later when you're not so attached to what your mind wants.

Healing a Broken Heart

At some point in your life you've probably heard someone (maybe yourself) say, "I gave my heart, and he hurt me." This implies that a sensitive emotional connection was hurt.

When that occurs, it's often hard for someone who hurt you to do anything to make it up. In most cases, you don't want to be heart vulnerable with the person. You want to protect yourself. It's up to you to do something yourself to heal the hurt.

This is where you need heart power to forgive, let go, and understand that it was the other person's lack of awareness that caused your hurt. Forgiveness is a core heart feeling that helps to release and heal the hurt so you can move on. Forgiveness helps you go deeper inside your heart to understand that it's never your real love that has been hurt or betrayed, but your expectations, attachments, and desires.

When your self-worth gets crushed, it's only human to feel that you were entitled to better. Your broken desires can turn into guilt, thinking you didn't do enough and therefore you deserved the hurt you got. You linger in "would've, could've, should've" thought loops. If you let regret and guilt consume you, it traps you in shame and self-blame. Too often, regret and guilt create a hiding place where you don't have to care anymore. That keeps you locked in self-blame and drains the energy you need to create a better future.

You can't change the past, yet guilt can tie you down with strings to the past, often causing you to repeat the very behavior you need to free yourself from while blocking you from perceiving new opportunities. Freeing yourself from the prison of guilt requires forgiveness of yourself and others.

Cut-Thru Exercise for Heartbreak

Cut-Thru is especially helpful for healing from heartache or heartbreak. If you are still healing from heartache or heartbreak, try the following when you practice Cut-Thru. Take it in phases.

Phase I: Find Peace and Compassion for Yourself

Genuinely become aware of *how you feel*. Do you feel hurt, angry, confused, and sad? Focus in the heart and solar plexus: *breathe love, appreciation,* and *compassion* for thirty seconds or up to three minutes. Continue this step until you feel some bit of calm and the beginnings of a more even internal rhythm.

Assume objectivity about the feeling or issue—as if it were someone else's problem. This is a very important step for heartbreak. Here is where you can really start picking up the pieces. Pretend you are watching another person feeling the hurt, not you. You may notice that you feel more compassion for and understanding of how he or she feels. Some find that, with this step, they want to hold and comfort this person. In your heart, you can. Embrace that hurt part of yourself with care, as if it were your own mother, father, child, or best friend. Compassion can soothe the painful feelings, like dipping a burn into cool water.

Increasing objectivity allows your feeling world to begin to ease toward neutral, to realize that there may be a bigger picture here, one that contains a spark of hope. *Rest in neutral*—in your rational, mature heart. *Soak and relax* in the compassion of the heart, dissolving the hurt a little at a time. If you are in overwhelming pain, you may need to spend time with these last few steps over several days before you go on to phase II. How long you take depends on you, but don't linger too long in phase I.

Phase II: Release—Letting Go and Moving On

Start again from Cut-Thru step 1 (described in chapter 9) and be prepared to mean business. As you revisit step 4, focus on a deeper neutral feeling and on finding a more rational, and sober, mature heart. Then as you go through step 5, don't just soak the hurt out—really soak the significance too. Few things feel as significant as heartbreak, but remember that wounded self-worth can be behind much of that significance. What is important to your recovery is your ability to forgive and release what your mind has been insisting should have happened instead.

From your deep heart sincerely ask for appropriate guidance or insight. The understandings your heart can deliver are always valuable, but when you are "up against the wall" they are worth more than their weight in gold. Honor and appreciate whatever glimmer of light you find, and write it down in your notebook to make it a new reference point.

Embracing Forgiveness

Forgiveness is one of the most powerful core heart feelings that you can send to yourself or others during Heart Lock-In or Cut-Thru practice. It is probably the most potent attitude for restoring mental, emotional, and spiritual health. Yet forgiveness is one of the hardest feelings to sustain, which is why we introduce this core heart feeling after you've learned the heart tools and techniques.

Forgiveness as an act of duty is not effective. It can leave you feeling as if you've done some good but this can mask over the problem rather than release it. "I know I should forgive" is not the same as forgiving if there is no genuine feeling behind it. It lacks the sincere heart intent and commitment to release someone cleanly at mental, emotional, and cellular levels. It's important to also let go of the idea of forgiving to *do someone else a favor.* Practice forgiveness for your sake, not for someone else's—for the sake of your own health, well-being, and future.

As issues come up that need forgiveness or self-forgiveness during your Heart Lock-In or Cut-Thru practice, shift to sending out forgiveness as an energy to yourself and the others involved, and really spend time in step 5, Soak and Relax, dissolving and taking out the significance to release the hurt, guilt, or resentment.

Events that have caused the deepest hurts can seem so unfair and unforgivable. You may decide to forgive and start the process, but soon the same nagging and painful feelings of anger or breach of trust creep back in—sometimes stronger than before.

To forgive, you need to dislodge your judgments, even before you fully understand why things happened. But most people want to understand why someone wronged them before they forgive. It's a catch-22 situation. This is what makes forgiveness so difficult and why people so often fail at it. After a while it seems easier to live in a state of pout or resentment than to try the forgiveness process again.

Forgiveness needs to be repeated until it reaches completion. Here's what can happen. Someone hurts you with words or deeds. After time has healed the pain somewhat, you decide to forgive them and you believe you have. Later you see the person do the same thing—and wham! It *retriggers* the cellular memory of what you'd already forgiven them for. You relive the same hurt and betrayed feelings you previously experienced. You judge them again, perhaps with even more vengeance. This is happening right now to thousands of people.

To forgive is a process that starts with heart vulnerability toward yourself. Use the Heart Lock-In technique, sending out an attitude of forgiveness to your cells and to the people or issues involved. Judgments may pop in that you haven't completely released at the feeling level, but as you maintain the emotional commitment to keep sending forgiveness, you will start to draw in more power from your spirit and more intuitive understanding. Long-standing memories of yesterday's resentments and feelings of unfairness may keep resurfacing. They are coming up to be resolved and released. Use the Cut-Thru technique, with forgiveness as the issue, and genuinely ask your heart with meaningfulness to help you forgive. Keep cutting through unresolved feelings with forgiveness for the other person, for yourself, or for life.

Forgiving yourself can be hardest. Often people tell themselves that they must keep remembering what they did wrong and beating themselves up for it or they will not learn. The opposite is true. Through genuine forgiveness, the wrong releases its emotional stranglehold on you so that you can see more clearly from a deeper heart intuition. That's what allows you to learn from it and change.

At times your heart will nudge you to talk to the person you are trying to forgive. This can be especially challenging. When it's someone you love or whose approval you still want, you have to overcome fear of rejection and fear of being judged. Be sincere in the heart before you speak. Have the courage to tell the person that you are afraid he or she may judge you and why.

Whatever their response, stay neutral in the heart and express yourself authentically. Don't clam up as you try to reconcile your differences. This act of heart vulnerability and courage ushers your spirit in to give you more intuitive understanding. Whether you come away closer to the person or realize that he is not going to change, use the opportunity to gain more heart empowerment to release fear, forgive, and let go. If the person is no longer in your life or has passed away, you can still talk with them in your heart and forgive them. Forgiveness for forgiveness' sake aligns your heart, mind, emotions, and cells in *amplified* coherence. Your entire system moves into a new rhythm of synchronicity and alignment with your spirit.

The Crucible of the Heart

Depression is often caused by past or current relationship issues and therefore can only be cured by resolving those conflicts within yourself. The first relationship is the relationship between your mind and heart. That's the first relationship conflict to be resolved, before you can truly resolve issues with another person. The heart has the strength to show you how to use heartache to become more of your real self. This often means loving and allowing another person to go his or her own way. Appreciate the depth of your experience and what you are learning. Appreciate the other person for having been part of your growth.

Life often seems exquisitely designed to teach each human being, in the crucible of the heart, that lasting fulfillment never comes from another. Security and the fulfillment of love come from within your heart, and you have to unfold that in yourself. Other people are gifts along the way.

chapter 11

Releasing Emotional Identities

Transforming depression is really about releasing emotional identities. Your *core self* is who you really are and really want to be. As you grow up and experience life, you develop layers around your core self that form not just one, but many different emotional identities. It's important to understand that releasing emotional identity is not about correcting something that is bad or wrong. Building identity is part of the human experience, and releasing those identities is about rediscovering who you really are.

Learning to be your real self means learning how to free yourself from layers of acquired identities that exist like shells around your core self. These shells influence who you think you are or should be. They shape your neural circuitry, your patterns of perception, your reactions, and your vanities in life. For most people, a lot of emotional energy is locked up in these identities.

Most emotional identities are based on the experiences you've had and the things your parents, friends, or society told you—what we call *hand-me-down beliefs* (about race, religion, politics, social status, and so forth). It's understandable that people born into different cultures or religions would have different hand-me-down beliefs. But when you become invested in hand-me-down beliefs and the emotional vanities they can create, they block you from hearing what your heart really knows.

When we speak of vanities, we're not talking about primping in front of the mirror or doing things to look better. We're talking about comparisons that put you above or below in relation to others (for example, "I'm better than you" or "I'll never be good enough"). We're also talking about jealousies, the need to be right, the need for approval, and other self-worth issues.

Many vanities are built on an overidentity with approval. Trying to get approval can feel like a way to build self-esteem, but actually it can undermine your ability to trust your own heart intelligence for approval and security. Often looking for outside approval turns into an emotional vanity where you do things purely for the approval of others with the hope of boosting your self-worth or your social status. Overidentification with approval can cause you to pursue career ambitions that aren't what your heart really wants.

The common urge to accumulate status symbols, such as high-paying jobs, luxury cars, or beautiful clothes, can be motivated by emotional vanity. There's nothing wrong with wanting these things, but if you become distraught if you don't get what you want, it's because of an overidentity consuming you. If you are not in touch with your deepest heart, the stimulation of approval and respect that other people give you in response to those status symbols can seem worthwhile, at least temporarily.

The truth is, when you attempt to base your sense of worth on the approval of others, you build shells of emotional identities around your core self. These identities create a self-centeredness that shuts off part of your heart to who *you* really are. When aspects of your heart shut down, you stifle nurturing from your own spirit. Gradually, a funk accumulates in your feeling world that snuffs out your potential for real love and diminishes the textures of appreciation and joy you could be experiencing.

Observing Identity and Vanity Motivations

Social pressures encourage people to build identities that compromise their real feelings and cloak their feelings with judgments. They allow people to judge themselves or others but not call it a judgment because it's "just the way things are." This seems so natural because everyone else is doing it or because someone you love is doing it. But it doesn't feel right to your deepest heart.

Have you ever cared so much about what others thought of you that you did something you didn't want to do or *didn't* do something you wanted to do—and later regretted it? That's an example of how emotional identity with what others think can create overcare and drive your decision. Almost everyone has had this experience more than once.

Have you ever desired something out of ambition or for glamour (a relationship, job, car, house, clothes, or expensive item)? When you finally got it, did you find it was unfulfilling and wonder why you'd ever invested so much time, energy, or money in pursuing it? That's an example of overidentity and vanity driving your desires. When you let emotional identities and vanities run your life, you can end up overwhelmed, sad, and, often, depressed.

This is deep psychology, but it's something that your heart can help you understand. As you practice the heart tools and techniques, your heart intelligence will reveal to you the identity and vanity drivers that motivate your attitudes and decisions. As you replace insecurity with security by operating more from your real heart, then seeing your hand-me-down beliefs, identity and vanity motivations in action becomes interesting, and even fascinating. Once you gain that objective view, you start to realize that you don't need a particular vanity or identity any longer. You will release these shells in stages as you build real self-security through making more heart-intelligent choices.

No one is going to take out all identities or vanities overnight. It took years to acquire them. You will fall back into old motives and patterns. When you do, just use a tool to reconnect with your core heart feelings and real care. If you beat yourself up for "doing it again" or "not having learned," that's just another vanity—expecting yourself to be perfect. Take the significance and identity out of that expectation, and just move back to your heart with dignity and integrity.

As you approach your learning process with understanding and compassion, you invite yourself to become more of your true self. You will increasingly bring in more spirit and find more security and peace in your heart as you learn to pull the emotional identification out of everything that isn't your real heart or core self.

Approval Vanity

Since approval needs are so often underneath an overidentity, it's important to take a deeper look at how they may be influencing you. You can see that approval insecurity is creating vanity when your thoughts are ruled by what others might think: "They'll like me better if I say this" or "What will they think of me if I choose this over that?" or "If I do this, he might be mad at me." Remember, this is so standard and it's not bad.

But overidentity about what others may think will block your real heart intuition from expressing itself in your thoughts.

When you depend on approval from outside, you compromise your power and intelligence inside. There's nothing wrong with external approval. It feels good and can motivate you to stay on track. But when you crave approval to validate your self-worth, you give your power away. An emotional, vanity-driven craving can provoke an endless cycle of worry that you aren't "good enough" if your approval need isn't fed. If someone criticizes you, it can prick your vanity and drain you emotionally for hours or days.

Approval vanity can also show up in an opposite way. Some people take the stance that they don't need approval from anyone, or they say, "I'm my own person and I don't care what anyone thinks about me." But, ironically, that's just an inverted approval vanity turned into a self-righteous vanity. That's very different from living in a secure place in the heart of not needing, but enjoying and appreciating others' approval. As you use the heart tools, you will build that secure place inside. You will learn to recognize the difference in quality between true feelings of security and all kinds of identities and vanities masquerading as security.

Learning the difference yourself can help you teach these skills to children, as well. In raising children, it takes heart intuition to find the balance between encouraging children through approval and reinforcing their budding vanities to the point where they become addicted to approval from parents and then from peers. When you constantly give children approval or rewards for every little thing, eventually the gifts have less meaning. That's what the word "spoiled" implies. When children get so used to getting, they develop a vanity of entitlement and can't find peace when life doesn't go their way. They've learned to rely on outside approval for their sense of identity and self-worth. You can help them develop self-security by teaching them to stay in touch with their own hearts.

Ambition Vanity

In a society obsessed with ambition and "being somebody," millions build their identities on acquiring money, possessions, and recognition, thinking these will bring them prestige and happiness. People are taught that ambition is good, but when they get overidentified and overinvested in ambition and it starts to run their lives, that cuts off a certain heart connection within their family relationships. That's when spouses go to marriage counselors.

When we talk about ambition here, we're not talking about the fun of going for something or having a passion for a goal. As people go to their hearts and look at the difference between ambition to achieve a goal and ambition as an obsession where the heart will get cut off somewhere, they can see where they may be creating a problem. So many times, ambition crosses a line and owns them. It takes heart intuition and discernment to know the dance. Once ambition starts to own people, then the heart feeling in relationships starts running thin and results in lots of time, anguish, and, often, money spent on trying to solve the problems created. Seeing the approval vanity and ambition vanity underlying the problems is often the bailout.

Brent's story illustrates this. Brent, a sales executive, was asked to write a book. He said he was filled with ambition:

> [I had] ambitions of becoming a published author, having reviews of my work in publications around the world, being interviewed on TV and radio about my brilliant ideas, being able to command high speaking fees, and finally gaining the

attention and approval I deserved. A preoccupation with the vanity of wanting to "be somebody" drove me during the eighteen months I was writing the book.

At the same time, I noticed what felt like a thinning of my spirit and a distance in my relationships with friends and coworkers. I started to feel sad and pushed it aside until I couldn't ignore the fact that I was depressed a lot of the time. I couldn't understand why I felt this way, since I was pursuing such a worthy ambition of writing a book to help others achieve success.

I was introduced to the Cut-Thru technique by a friend who told me it would help me understand what was really going on. I saw that I had a strong drive for recognition and it was cutting me off from others. I asked my heart to bring me a deeper connection with my real self, beyond the public expression of it. My heart told me to relax and spend more time with the people I care about in my life and forget about myself for a while. I did that and took a break from writing for several months. When I went back to the book, I experienced a profound shift. There was a new sense of purpose and love about what I was writing and a much deeper care for the people who would be helped by the book, without the glamour of recognition driving me.

Approval insecurities will cause you to shape your ambitions and define success by how the outside world sees you. The heart defines success as the expression of your real self. As you practice the heart tools, your life will become a reflection of your ever-deepening heart connection with your real self and with others. Ambition will turn into creative expression of heart and mind. Recognition, if it comes, will be an add-on, not something you need.

Performance Vanity

A lot of approval vanity is related to performance. Sue's practice of Cut-Thru revealed a lot of performance vanity in her personal life.

When I stopped to look at my background thoughts—the ones that always seem to be there—the themes went like this: Am I a good enough mother? Shouldn't I be doing more for my son? Am I a good enough lover to my husband? Will he find someone else more spontaneous and attractive than me? It went on and on, and all I wanted to do was go to the fridge and eat whatever sweets I could find to ease the feeling and take care of myself. I really knew better and my heart said everything was alright, that I didn't need to worry, but these insecure thoughts kept taking over, and I was really depressed.

If you have background thoughts and feelings similar to Sue's, realize this is very common. A large percentage of people feel different aspects of this, and it's an energy drain. You're not a special case. It's when these thoughts and feelings become consuming that they can lead to depression. The way you deal with them is to "take the significance out" when they come up. Take it on as a project, and they will start to go away. It's like feeding the neighborhood cat. If you stop feeding him, he'll go away. Sure people have tried time and again to deal with obsessive thoughts and feelings. But it's their mind that has tried. As people learn more about the power of their heart and intuition to cut through thought and feeling loops, it opens up a new playing field to get more mileage out of their efforts and get results.

Sue's therapist suggested that she practice Cut-Thru and the heart tools for thirty days to see if she could release those thoughts and fears that had a stranglehold on her.

*After a week of practice, I was able to catch when the
performance thoughts started and fold them into my heart.
Each time I did that, I felt a lessening of the thoughts and
I felt more centered. They didn't go away, but they were
quieter. My heart gave me strength and encouragement.
I saw that these thoughts were my own fabrications and I
didn't need to believe them. They came from an insecurity
I'd had since I was a child, where my parents constantly told
me that I didn't do things good enough.*

*I used the Cut-Thru technique once a day on this old
identity and Attitude Breathing with replacement attitudes
each time the thoughts and anxieties would come up as I
was moving through my day. I kept telling myself "take
the significance out" when they'd come up. At the end of
thirty days, I didn't feel they were controlling me anymore.
Oh, they still try to come up, but I know they aren't me.
I say "No" and bring in my replacement attitudes. My
relationships with my husband and son are so much better,
and that encourages me to keep using the tools. The cherry
on top is that I've even lost five pounds.*

Comparison Vanity

Approval or performance vanity can also drive a need to
compare yourself with others to assess your self-worth. People
who live or work together often feel jealous of one another's
capabilities. These jealousies usually lurk in a secret, stored
feeling world while everyone pretends to get along. You can
think someone else is doing better than you, and self-pity
thoughts set in, like "I'm trying, but poor me, I'm not there
yet" or "It's unfair that things seem to be a little harder for me
than for others, but don't get me wrong—I appreciate the work
I've done" or "I appreciate myself and all I have, but I don't
really deserve it." Underlying these thoughts are feelings of

what's fair or unfair, which turn into judgments and blame. As approval insecurities create comparisons, you can seesaw up and down between vanity extremes of self-importance and false humility. You feel puffed up when you assess you're doing well, and you feel down and out when you think you're doing poorly. Again, these insecurities and emotional identities are so standard in human beings that they are nothing to be critical of or to feel bad about. It's just that for your own mental health and empowerment, you don't need to remain their victim.

Effectiveness in life has nothing to do with vanity comparisons. It's not talent or position that brings happiness. This is why people who are highly talented often don't have any more peace or better relationships than people who aren't. Talents or the lack of them do not determine your quality of life. Effectiveness at being yourself is what brings you peace of mind and heart. If someone else is more skilled at speaking, writing, or golfing than you, you can be secure in yourself and happy that they're talented in their own way.

Some people have a need to be right, a need to control, or a need to be perfect. These are based on underlying and often unconscious insecurities that something is wrong with them or that they are lesser than others if they aren't in control or aren't right. These are often beliefs that have grown from parental expectations. For some people, "perfect" means being perfect in a role: the perfect daughter, father, wife, mother, husband, student, employee, or friend. For others, the need to be perfect becomes an obsession about looks—the perfect body, hair, or clothes. When you are obsessed with being perfect, you strive for an ideal you can never reach, and that can depress you. Or if something topples your self-image, you can end up sliding into depression.

In reality, there is no such thing as "perfect." People are always doing things more or less effectively until they learn to do them better. The same is true in learning to understand yourself and to listen to and follow your heart. Learn to measure your progress in ratios, like three steps forward and two back, and then try to improve your ratio. That way you build in latitude and make the process of freeing yourself from emotional identities smoother.

Good Getting in the Way

What we call *good getting in the way* is what some people get most upset about in themselves. They try to "do good" and then feel unappreciated for their efforts or that life has been unfair. This can lead to a feeling of victimization and blame: "But I did all this for you." Good getting in the way is common in relationships, workplaces, and social causes. People take on extra work at their jobs or for a cause when their heart is saying it's really time to do something else for balance in life. Yet they strain to keep going and soldier all the stress because "they're good." Their hearts keep signaling it's time to make a change, but they are so identified with the good that they're doing that it overrides the courage to do what's best. This often continues until they have a mental, emotional, or physical breakdown. The solution is not to give up the desire to do good but to consider how to turn "good" into effectiveness. Otherwise doing good will remain a storefront for a lot of stress, overwhelming feelings, and depression.

If good getting in the way is your issue, take time-outs during the day to ask your heart: "What is the best attitude of care for myself and others (without overcare) that I could have right now?" Listen to your heart and make a sincere heart effort to shift to that attitude. This will realign you with your deeper heart. Then ask your heart, "What would be the most appropriate action of care to take right now?" Listen to whatever commonsense direction your heart shows you, and act on it.

✐ Cut-Thru Exercise to Release Emotional Identity

To develop inner security and be your real self, you need to release hand-me-down beliefs and emotional identities that are holding you back. This is an unfolding process. You may experience resistance, dread, or anxiety that you won't be okay if you let go of them. This insecurity is also standard and not bad. Have compassionate understanding that you are releasing identities that built your approach to life but which you are now outgrowing. Have compassion that people everywhere are being asked to let go of old identities and grow up in the shift energies on the planet. When you feel a strong insecurity, resistance, or dread, try the following exercise.

Step 1. Do a Heart Lock-In and send ease and compassion to soothe your system. Ask your heart: what is the belief or emotional identity underneath the resistant or obstinate feeling? Go deeper in your heart to the truth in your feeling world. Be honest about what you see. It won't bite you. Let go of the sense that something's bad, and enfold whatever you feel or see into the heart. *Soak and relax* in the compassion of the heart, dissolving the significance a little at a time.

Step 2. *Assume objectivity* about the feeling or issue—as if it were someone else's problem. Send compassion to "that other person." This objectivity allows your feeling world to begin to ease toward neutral. *Rest in neutral*—in your rational, mature heart.

Step 3. Ask your heart for a replacement attitude and breathe that attitude for a while to increase coherence and to anchor a new attitude into your system. This will release some of the old identity and bring in more of your real spirit—the real you. Just let the old dense feelings spin off, and know that they are *not* you. Hold to your heart intent, take the significance out, and gradually those dense feelings will loosen and release, even if it takes a while. Listen to your heart and follow your heart, especially if it prompts you to communicate vulnerably from the heart with family or friends.

The answer to releasing identities and vanities is to move from *muddling* through to *cutting* through. This process of clearing layers of long-standing beliefs and emotionally invested identities can feel threatening to your modus operandi. You may have developed a quick-reacting defensiveness in self-protection. Keep filtering defensiveness out through the heart, and it will ease so you can see more clearly. Use the tools to release resistances, and the beauty of your real self will emerge from behind the facade of defensiveness.

As you become more secure in your heart, you will find that operating from old motives and identities will start to feel awkward. It won't feel right to your heart any longer because you're outgrowing them. You'll say, "No, I see where that motivation is coming from and where it will lead, and I'm not going to do that."

Most people can look back at their lives and remember issues they once supported (where they now support the opposite perspective) or relationships that felt so right at first. Later, however, they saw that misplaced beliefs or ambitions had motivated them. People either mature from these realizations and make more heart-intelligent choices going forward, or they keep repeating the same old choices from hand-me-down beliefs and identities and have the same dissatisfying outcomes.

Depression frequently results from repeated dissatisfy-ing experiences and not understanding why the same thing always happens. As you use the Cut-Thru technique, you will unravel the mystery of why the same things keep happening to you. You will discover your identity drivers that keep creat-ing similar situations. As you understand them, you will be able to release them from heart intelligence and start to create situations that bring you more fulfilling outcomes.

Heart Approval—Growing Up

Ultimately, only the heart can give people the approval and security they need. The heart sends messages of approval throughout the body, through different glands, hormones, neurotransmitters, and other messenger molecules confirming your choices. But often, before they can do their work, those messages become clouded.

The heart gives signals when you're going a different direc-tion than your heart intelligence would want, but you have to know how to listen to those signals. Sometimes they come as a stress feeling or an inner voice of conscience that says no or in different ways that you learn to recognize as you act on the signal and see the beneficial outcome. These signals from your heart intelligence are intended to align you with your core self and with whatever would be the best for yourself and for the whole, whether you understand it yet or not. Often you can't see the bigger picture until you go down the road a bit. As you learn to sense and follow your heart's intuitive signals, then see how those heart choices play out positively in life, you come to trust your heart.

People mature in stages in learning to listen to and follow their heart. The first stage starts with confusion between what the head (rational mind, beliefs, identities, vanity motives) and the heart (inspiration, a feeling or hunch, intuition) are saying. There can be a mistrust of the heart's signals. (Is it really my heart intuition? How can I be sure? What if I just made it up?) Your heart can come online and say, "Let go, everything will be all right. It's never as bad as you think it is," dismissing your mind's concerns. Your mind may say, "Oh sure, how can that be?" and go back to its old thoughts, as if you'd turned the dial on a radio back to an old station.

Learning any skill, whether it's a musical instrument, a sport, or computer programming, takes practice. The heart tools give you the practice you need to develop and fine-tune your heart skills. Your heart will give you approval signals throughout the process.

Appreciating your progress and giving yourself approval for doing what your heart tells you—having the courage to communicate authentically, achieving a goal, or coming up with a creative idea—will build healthy self-worth that no one can take away from you. It's when your mind overidentifies with an achievement that self-importance can seep in, putting you up in comparison to others and causing a low-grade righteousness to flow through your emotional energetics. This creates separation from your heart and from others. You may then wonder why people aren't as approving of you as you are of yourself.

As you practice the heart tools, you'll see that mind rationalizations *feel* different than heart intuition. As you build the coherent alignment between your heart and mind, you will be able to ask questions of your heart and get intuitive answers that seem to have a higher order of intelligence and refinement. Aligning the power of the mind with the power of the heart unlocks creativity. You hone your creative problem-solving skills and start to attract more people, situations, and events that are fulfilling to your heart and mind. You draw more of your real heart's desires to you as you feel more secure in following your heart.

When you really want something badly, you can think the desire is from your heart and not see the overidentity or over-attachment driving it. Wanting something too much from the mind creates a static, so you can't *tune in* to your deeper heart's want.

To find your deeper heart, take the mental and emotional energy out of the "want" and release it to the heart. That allows your intuition to show you the heart's want, which may not be the same as your emotional desire. Most often a true heart's desire has a balance and ease along with passion.

Living in the Heart

Learning to live in the heart and manage your energies from the heart is an empowering and enlightening process. It progressively unfolds your greatest potentials. As you use the heart tools, you come to appreciate all of your past experiences as part of your learning and growing. A balanced approach to growth requires appreciating yourself not only when things are going well, but especially when you have a setback. Appreciate whatever progress you make, and then use that energy of appreciation to move forward. Recognize that to dwell in poor-me attitudes or unfair feelings is a convenient hiding place, but it holds you back. Have compassion for yourself and embrace your humanness.

Whenever you experience breakthroughs on issues related to identity, you have to walk steadily in the new realization to keep anchoring your new insights. Each insight is a gift to pay attention to, or it can fade. This requires walking steadily in the light of the new. Do it from integrity, not out of fear that you'll regress.

You may wonder who you will be without the comfort zone of the layers you've built up around your real self through the years. It takes the power of the heart and love to cut through the layers. That's what love is designed to do—to make you whole. Through love and love alone, a new identity with your real self emerges.

Your true identity or core self is love. Your higher potential finds you when you set your course in that direction. Living in the heart is approving yourself, and it releases you from identities and vanities so that you unfold your real self—free of the shells of limiting patterns, free to love without fear. As philosopher Pierre Teilhard de Chardin said, "The conclusion is always the same: Love is the most powerful and still the most unknown energy in the world."

chapter 12

Heart-Based Living

Preventing and transforming depression in today's world can be greatly facilitated by learning to reopen and live more from the heart. There is power and intelligence in the heart to help people do that. This book has been a step-by-step process on how to connect with that power and access the intelligence of the heart to release and prevent depression.

Shifting from a depressive perspective to a freeing insight is like changing a radio dial to a different station. Heart power gives you the ability to turn the dial. The HeartMath tools offer you practical new ways to find those insights to free yourself from depression.

Putting It All Together

People have been seeking clear answers from their heart's intelligence for thousands of years. Today, more and more people are beginning to discover the power of the heart. It's part of a new momentum of heart intelligence unfolding on the planet.

The world-renowned neuroscientist, Dr. Karl Pribram, who directed Stanford's Neuropsychology Laboratory for thirty years, explains how focusing in the area of the heart and feeling love, appreciation, or care is like adding a lens to the heart's system. He says,

> *You've got to have eyes to see, you've got to have the heart to feel. The "lens" of positive heart feelings, like love, care, and appreciation, brings you intuitive perception. Love increases coherence and clarity. When you use tools like Cut-Thru and Heart Lock-In to stop all the nonsense (mental and emotional nonsense) for a while, it's like focusing the lens of heart perception.*

The heart provides the lens through which you can decipher the language of your feeling world more consistently and see life more completely. Increasing people's understanding of how this works is a core mission of the Institute of HeartMath.

Trying to resolve emotional issues with cognitive efforts alone won't work for clearing most depression. The cognitive mind does not have the power to manage the emotions. So it comes down to the heart. That's why we created the Heart-Math tools. The intelligence accessed by the heart is designed to help people manage and resolve their emotional issues.

As you have seen throughout this book, emotional energy is real energy. It moves faster than the speed of thought. The earlier chapters have shown you what you need to do for emotional energetics maintenance. These principles and tools will allow you to minimize the anxiety and overload that can induce low-grade or major depression. You are either accumulating emotional stress and draining energy or managing your emotions and gaining energy. By practicing the techniques in this book, you can develop the empowerment you need to manage your emotions—even if you think it isn't possible or don't know how.

Empowerment is a progressive and unfolding process of using your heart intelligence to *not* get hooked back into old thought loops and emotional impulses. Empowerment allows you to build new memory references so you can follow your heart intelligence with increasing consistency.

When you start any new practice, you always hope for immediate results. You may worry that you won't do the practice correctly, that it won't work for you, or that it's not as effective as it was said to be. Put aside these concerns. Allow yourself to ease into this new process rather than trying to take it by storm. The art of easing in helps you connect to your heart and accomplish what you couldn't do before.

Review of Tools and Techniques

As stress keeps increasing in the world, people will have to upgrade their own psychology and add more meaningfulness to their lives. Emotional energy responsibility is the new solution that people have to learn to keep pace with the speedup of life.

Notice and Ease and Power of Neutral

As you use Notice and Ease and Power of Neutral (see pages 32 and 34), you will literally regrid your emotional response system to clear reactions as you go and prevent stress accumulation. Remember that emotional reactions are faster than your mind's intentions, so use these two tools along with the Quick Coherence technique (see page 59) to get ahead of the triggers.

When you learn to go to your deeper heart, you will have even more coherent power at these hinge points. With practice, you will learn to make different choices and develop greater intuitive discernment.

Attitude Breathing

Attitude Breathing (see page 82) is an invaluable technique to help you stop repeating negative downward spirals when something gets to you. It's designed to *take the significance out* of whatever has come up.

With Attitude Breathing, you can reset your patterns to a new baseline, empowering your physiology to work for you. Otherwise the strong negative attitude pattern of depression will bring back the old cellular imprints that encourage you to dwell on previous disappointments and blame. You don't want to start reprocessing those again and stacking more negative energy on top of a current issue you haven't cleared.

Make a list of your best attitude replacements. Practice Attitude Breathing with them throughout the day, whether or not you are feeling stressed. Breathe these replacement attitudes in order to have core heart feelings running through your system. This preventive maintenance will help offset a lot of overcare, overidentity, or overattachment that may come up during the day. So much overwhelm and depression can be prevented by learning how to clear as you go and committing to do that. At least commit to avoiding the things that you know will drain and cause a setback. Make a commitment to making attitude shifts and anchoring in new attitudes on those issues.

Heart Lock-In and Cut-Thru

Use the Heart Lock-In technique (see page 96) for five minutes or longer several times a week to learn how to sustain coherence, for longer time periods, increase your energy levels, and accelerate healing.

Use the Cut-Thru technique (see page 119) on major issues you are dealing with and on mental and emotional thought loops that keep recurring. Cut-Thru practice is an unfolding process of gaining the releases and intuitive insights you need for recovery.

Dealing with long-term depression is challenging. We all know there is no quick fix. At HeartMath we have also seen the amazing effectiveness of these tools, over and over again. You can regain your hope and power of intent and make remarkable changes.

Take Things in Sections

After you have sincerely practiced the heart tools and techniques for a few weeks, go back and look at your scores on the Depression Checklist from chapter 1.

Score yourself again to see if any of your numbers have changed or if your perspectives have changed. Appreciate any improvements you see. Look at your answers to the questions in the section How the Planetary Shift Is Affecting You at the end of chapter 2. Write down any new insights you have now. Revisit these two exercises periodically in order to keep track of your progress.

Ask your heart intuition which issues to apply the tools to, now that you've learned the basics. Use your heart intuition to identify what to address next. Take issues in sections, one at a time. Don't try to address everything all at once. There will be times when you aren't sure if it's your heart or mind guiding you. But through practicing the Heart Lock-In and Cut-Thru techniques, especially, you'll increasingly be able to track what's going on in your mind and emotions and shift to heart coherence to gain a growing intuitive understanding.

Heart Coherence Technology

You can train yourself to increase your coherence levels even more quickly with heart rhythm coherence technology. Heart-Math's portable emWave Personal Stress Reliever and the computer-based emWave PC Stress Relief System will monitor and display your changing heart rhythm (heart rate variability) patterns and coherence levels *in real time*. When you're feeling overwhelmed, sad, or stressed, you can use a heart tool and watch your heart rhythm pattern shift into more coherence. You get immediate feedback in the context you need it, to motivate self-management and emotional energy responsibility. Using heart coherence technology helps you build a cushion of flexibility, making it easier to say, "No, I'm not going to react the same old way" rather than falling into your standard patterns of emotional persuasion. This will help reset your patterns more quickly.

Health Professionals Use HeartMath

Many psychiatrists, psychologists, and other health professionals are using HeartMath tools and heart coherence technology in their practices. Many of the stories in this book were provided by licensed HeartMath providers. Charly Cungy, MD, a psychiatrist in France, specializes in using Heart-Math tools to treat patients with clinical depression. One of his patients, Peter, changed his schema (problematic beliefs and overidentities) and recovered from major depression in just a few months. Peter maintained his recovery at both his six-month and one-year follow-up evaluations. You can find Peter's case study, along with his pre- and postassessments, at www.heartmath.org.

As the World Shifts

Depressive attitudes and moods create a big filter between you and your heart. Temporary or long-term, depression takes people into a lonely place of self-absorption. If you multiply your own anxieties, overcares, overattachments, and overidentities by six billion people on the planet—many of whom are experiencing an overload of similar feelings—it's easy to see why depression is becoming a global epidemic.

The speed at which the world is moving is speeding up emotional reactions and increasing stress levels. The incoherent electromagnetic energy that stress generates keeps old histories and triggers going off. Everyone has a bundle of old histories stored in their emotional systems. *Yet, this speedup of time, energy, and change can also be used to clear emotional histories faster.*

One of the upsides of this momentum of global change is that positive emotional changes can also happen more quickly. This energetic momentum is something to take advantage of *now*. As you increase your heart coherence levels, you'll have more leverage to shift your emotional responses to flow with the speed of change. Heart coherence creates a cushion between you and stressors that come up. Coherence increases your capacity to make nonstressful choices and brings clearer intuition on how to respond.

Deeper Care

It all gets down to deeper care. Using tools to generate core heart feelings that create coherence, like love, compassion, and appreciation, is all about deeper care. Deeper care stops emotional histories from repeating themselves and makes insight easier. Deeper care activates the intuition of the heart to provide new solutions, which are not accessible in an atmosphere of stress and incoherence.

By practicing the HeartMath tools, you will be able to shift your control to your heart. You will be able to manage your emotions, be responsible for your own energies, and build a bridge between your mind and heart. Instead of lingering in depression, you will become the architect of a new sense of hope and power within yourself. You will begin to live your core values, rather than just wishing you could.

As you practice the tools, the process will become faster and progressively more automatic. Eventually, without consciously using a tool, you will stay centered in a flow of heart intelligence for longer periods of time. It will feel awkward and uncomfortable to be out of touch with your heart.

This is the way of the future. Living in the heart is the key that will take us all beyond the information age to the age of heart-based living.

Learn More About HeartMath Products

Explore other HeartMath books, e-books, learning programs, music, software, seminars and professional training to reinforce and advance what you've learned in this book. More details can be found online at: http://heartmath.com.

Books and Learning Programs by Doc Childre

Childre, Doc and Bruce C. Wilson, MD, 2006. *The HeartMath Approach to Managing Hypertension: The Proven, Natural Way to Lower Your Blood Pressure.*

Childre, Doc and Deborah Rozman, 2006. *Transforming Anxiety: The HeartMath Solution for Overcoming Fear and Worry and Creating Serenity.*

Childre, Doc and Deborah Rozman, 2005. *Transforming Stress: The HeartMath Solution for Relieving Worry, Fatigue, and Tension.*

Childre, Doc and Deborah Rozman, 2003. *Transforming Anger: The HeartMath Solution for Letting Go of Rage, Frustration and Irritation*

Childre, Doc and Howard Martin, 1999. *The HeartMath Solution*. San Francisco, Harper San Francisco.

Childre, Doc and Bruce Cryer, 2000. *From Chaos to Coherence: The Power to Change Performance From Chaos to Coherence (CD-Rom)*, Boulder Creek, CA. HeartMath LLC and Knowl edgebuilder.com

Childre, Doc 1992. *The How to Book of Teen Self Discovery*, Boulder Creek, CA. Planetary Publications.

Music by Doc Childre

Scientifically designed to enhance the practice of HeartMath techniques and tools.

Heart Zone, Planetary Publications

Speed of Balance, Planetary Publications

Quiet Joy, Planetary Publications

emWave® PC Stress Relief System (formerly known as the Freeze-Framer®)

emWave PC is a patented interactive learning system with heart rhythm monitor and pulse sensor. This software-based program allows you to observe your heart rhythms in real time and assists you in increasing coherence to reduce stress and improve health and performance. The Coherence Coach, Emotion Visualizer, and three software games in emWave PC are fun ways to build your skills an emotional management.

emWave® Personal Stress Reliever®

emWave Personal Stress Reliever is a breakthrough in stress reduction technology. This stress reliever helps build a cushion between you and day-to-day stress, thereby enhancing energy and performance. A mobile device weighing just 2.2 ounces and small enough to fit in your pocket, you can take it with you to use anytime, anywhere.

emTech™ Media Products

emTech products were created by utilizing information from a variety of HeartMath resources. They offer some of the best subject-specific information found in the HeartMath System and are available as e-booklets, audio programs and interactive learning modules.

Test Edge™ Interactive CD-ROM— Grade 9-12 and above

This unique interactive learning program helps students balance their mental and emotional systems, which is critical for successful learning and test taking. Without emotional balance, feelings of anxiety and fear jam the connection between what students really know and what they can actually express, especially while taking tests. The TestEdge tools help students to clear disturbances they carry into the classroom from peer pressure, stress overload, problems at home or in relationships.

HeartMath Seminars and Training

HeartMath provides world-class training programs for organizations, hospitals, health care providers and individuals. HeartMath training is available through on-site programs, licensing and certification for organizations, and sponsored workshops, seminars and conference presentations.

Licensing and Certification - 1 on 1 Provider (Coaching)

HeartMath offers licensing and certification to health care providers, coaches and consultants wanting to use HeartMath tools and technology as part of the services they provide to clients in a one-on-one professional model.

Licensing and Certification: "Train the Trainer" Programs for Organizations

HeartMath also offers licensing and training to organizations wanting to make the HeartMath tools and technologies a part of their offerings to internal customers, employees, or members.

For information on products, seminars and workshops, call 1-800-450-9111, e-mail info@heartmath.com, visit the website at www .heartmath.com, or write to: HeartMath,14700 West Park Avenue, Boulder Creek, CA 95006

Research and Education

The Institute of HeartMath® (IHM) is a nonprofit research and education organization dedicated to understanding emotions and the role of the heart in learning, performance and well-being. IHM offers programs for use in educational and classroom settings:

TestEdge™ programs for improving academic performance and test scores, K-12.

Resiliency and Quality Instructor (QIP) programs for teachers, administrators and principals

http://www.heartmath.org
For information about Institute of HeartMath research papers, research initiatives and education programs, call 831-338-8500, e-mail: info@heartmath.org, visit the website at www.heartmath.org or write to: Institute of HeartMath 14700 West Park Avenue, Boulder Creek, CA 95006

References

Ardayfio, P., and K.-S. Kim. 2006. Anxiogenic-like effect of chronic corticosterone in the light-dark emergence task in mice. *Behavioral Neuroscience* 120(2):249–56.

Armour, J. A. 1991. Anatomy and function of the intrathoracic neurons regulating the mammalian heart. In *Reflex Control of the Circulation*, edited by I. H. Zucker and J. P. Gilmore, 1-37. Boca Raton, FL: CRC Press.

Armour, J. A., and G. C. Kember. 2004. Cardiac sensory neurons. In *Basic and Clinical Neurocardiology*, edited by J. A. Armour and J. L. Ardell, 79-117. New York: Oxford University Press.

Arnetz, B., and R. Ekman, eds. 2006. *Stress in Health and Disease*. Weinheim, Germany: Wiley-VCH.

Balogh, S., D. F. Fitzpatrick, S. E. Hendricks, and S. R. Paige. 1993. Increases in heart rate variability with successful treatment in patients with major depressive disorder. *Psychopharmacological Bulletin* 29(2):201–6.

Barrios-Choplin, B., R. McCraty, and B. Cryer. 1997. An inner quality approach to reducing stress and improving physical and emotional well-being at work. *Stress Medicine* 13(3):193–201.

Blehar, M. D., and D. A. Oren. 1997. Gender differences in depression. *Medscape Women's Health* 2(2):3.

Bower, B. 2006. Prescription for controversy: Medications for depressed kids spark scientific dispute. *Science News*, March 18.

Brody, J. 1998. Depression untreated in millions of elderly. *San Jose Mercury News*, November 11.

Cameron, O. G. 2002. *Visceral Sensory Neuroscience: Interoception.* New York: Oxford University Press.

Cantin, M., and J. Genest. 1986. The heart as an endocrine gland. *Scientific American* 254(2):76–81.

Carney, R. M., K. E. Freedland, P. K. Stein, J. A. Skala, P. Hoffman, and A. S. Jaffe. 2000. Change in heart rate and heart rate variability during treatment for depression in patients with coronary heart disease. *Psychosomatic Medicine* 62(5):639–47.

Centers for Disease Control and Prevention. 2006. *Surveillance Summaries*, June 9. MMWR 2006; 55 (No. SS-5): Table 16.

Dekker, J. M., E. G. Schouten, P. Klootwijk, J. Pool, C. A. Swenne, and D. Kromhout. 1997. Heart rate variability from short electrocardiographic recordings predicts mortality from all causes in middle-aged and elderly men. The Zutphen Study. *American Journal of Epidemiology* 145(10):899–908.

Dobbs, D. 2006. Turning off depression. *Scientific American Mind* 17(4):26–31.

Ford, D. E., L. A. Mead, P. P. Chang, L. Cooper-Patrick, N. Y. Wang, and M. J. Klag. 1998. Depression is a risk factor for coronary artery disease in men: The Precursors Study. *Archives of Internal Medicine* 158(13):1422–26.

Fredrickson, B. L. 2000. Cultivating positive emotions to optimize health and well-being. *Prevention & Treatment* 3(1), Article 0001a. http://content.apa.org/journals/pre/3/1/1.

———. 2001. The role of positive emotions in positive psychology. The broaden-and-build theory of positive emotions. *American Psychologist* 56(3):218–26.

———. 2002. Positive emotions. In *Handbook of Positive Psychology*, edited by C. R. Snyder and S. J. Lopez, 120–34. New York: Oxford University Press.

Frysinger, R. C., and R. M. Harper. 1990. Cardiac and respiratory correlations with unit discharge in epileptic human temporal lobe. *Epilepsia* 31(2):162–71.

Gershon, M. 1999. *The Second Brain*. San Francisco: Harper-Collins.

Goetzel, R. Z., D. R. Anderson, R. W. Whitmer, R. J. Ozminkowski, R. L. Dunn, and J. Wasserman. 1998. The relationship between modifiable health risks and health care expenditures. An analysis of the multi-employer HERO health risk and cost database. The Health Enhancement Research Organization (HERO) Research Committee. *Journal of Occupational and Environmental Medicine* 40(10):843–54.

Goldapple, K., Z. Segal, C. Garson, M. Lau, P. Bieling, S. Kennedy, and H. Mayberg. 2004. Modulation of cortical-limbic pathways in major depression: Treatment-specific effects of cognitive behavior therapy. *Archives of General Psychiatry* 61(1):34–41.

Gutkowska, J., M. Jankowski, S. Mukaddam-Daher, and S. M. McCann. 2000. Oxytocin is a cardiovascular hormone. *Brazilian Journal of Medical and Biological Research* 33:625–33.

Horwitz, A. V., and J. C. Wakefield. 2005. The age of depression. *Public Interest*, Winter.

Isen, A. M. 1999. Positive affect. In *Handbook of Cognition and Emotion*, edited by T. Dalgleish and M. Power, 522–39. New York: John Wiley & Sons.

Kerr, D. S., L. W. Campbell, M. D. Applegate, A. Brodish, and P. W. Landfield. 1991. Chronic stress-induced acceleration of electrophysiologic and morphometric biomarkers of hippocampal aging. *Journal of Neuroscience* 11(5):1316–24.

Kirsch, I., T. J. Moore, A. Scoboria, and S. S. Nicholls. 2002. The emperor's new drugs: An analysis of antidepressant medication data submitted to the U.S. Food and Drug Administration. *Prevention & Treatment* 5(1). http://content .apa.org/journals/pre/5/1/23.

LeDoux, J. 1996. *The Emotional Brain: The Mysterious Underpinnings of Emotional Life*. New York: Simon & Schuster.

Luskin, F., M. Reitz, K. Newell, T. G. Quinn, and W. Haskell. 2002. A controlled pilot study of stress management training of elderly patients with congestive heart failure. *Preventive Cardiology* 5(4):168–72.

Mayberg, H. S. 1997. Limbic-cortical dysregulation: A proposed model of depression. *Journal of Neuropsychiatry and Clinical Neurosciences* 9(3):471–81.

Mayberg, H. S., A. M. Lozano, V. Voon, H. E. McNeely, D. Seminowicz, C. Hamani, J. M. Schwalb, and S. H. Kennedy. 2005. Deep brain stimulation for treatment-resistant depression. *Neuron* 45(5):651–60.

McCraty, R. 2004. The energetic heart: Bioelectromagnetic communication within and between people. In *Bioelectromagnetic Medicine*, edited by P. J. Rosch and M. S. Markov, 541–62. New York: Marcel Dekker.

McCraty, R., M. Atkinson, and R. T. Bradley. 2004a. Electrophysiological evidence of intuition: Part 1. The surprising role of the heart. *Journal of Alternative and Complementary Medicine* 10(1):133–43.

———. 2004b. Electrophysiological evidence of intuition: Part 2. A system-wide process? *Journal of Alternative and Complementary Medicine* 10(2):325–36.

McCraty, R., M. Atkinson, W. A. Tiller, G. Rein, and A. D. Watkins. 1995. The effects of emotions on short-term power spectrum analysis of heart rate variability. *American Journal of Cardiology* 76(14):1089–93.

McCraty, R., M. Atkinson, and D. Tomasino. 2003. Impact of a workplace stress reduction program on blood pressure and emotional health in hypertensive employees. *Journal of Alternative and Complementary Medicine* 9(3):355–69.

McCraty, R., M. Atkinson, D. Tomasino, and R. T. Bradley. 2006. *The Coherent Heart: Heart-Brain Interactions, Psychophysiological Coherence, and the Emergence of System-Wide Order*. Publication No. 06–022. Boulder Creek, CA: HeartMath Research Center, Institute of HeartMath.

McCraty, R., and D. Tomasino. 2006. Emotional stress, positive emotions, and psychophysiological coherence. In *Stress in Health and Disease*, edited by B. B. Arnetz and R. Ekman, 342–65. Weinheim, Germany: Wiley-VCH.

Molinare, E., A. Compare, and G. Parati, eds. 2006. *Clinical Psychology and Heart Disease*. Milan: Springer.

Moncrieff, J., and D. Cohen. 2006. Do antidepressants cure or create abnormal brain states? *PLoS Medicine* 3(7):e240, doi: 10.1371/journal.pmed.0030240. http://medicine.plosjournals.org/archive/1549-1676/3/7/pdf/10.1371_journal.pmed.0030240-p-S.pdf.

Moncrieff, J., and I. Kirsch. 2005. Efficacy of antidepressants in adults. *British Medical Journal* 331(7509):155–57. http://www.bmj.com/cgi/reprint/331/7509/155

Murray, C. J. L., and A. D. Lopez. 1996. *The Global Burden of Disease: A Comprehensive Assessment of Mortality and Disability from Diseases, Injuries and Risk Factors in 1990 and Projected to 2020.* Cambridge, MA: Harvard University Press, on behalf of the World Health Organization and the World Bank.

Pace, T., T. Mletzko, O. Alagbe, D. Musselman, C. Nemeroff, A. Miller, and C. Heim. 2006. Increased stress-induced inflammatory responses in male patients with major depression and increased early life stress. *American Journal of Psychiatry* 163(9):1630–33.

Pribram, K. H., and F. T. Melges. 1969. Psychophysiological basis of emotion. In *Handbook of Clinical Neurology*, vol. 3, edited by P. J. Vinken and G. W. Bruyn, 316–41. Amsterdam: North-Holland Publishing Company.

Raz, A. 2006. Perspectives on the efficacy of antidepressants for child and adolescent depression. *PLoS Medicine* 3(1):e9, doi: 10.1371/journal.pmed.0030009. http://medicine.plosjournals.org/archive/1549-1676/3/1/pdf/10.1371_journal.pmed.0030009-S.pdf.

Rozanski, A., J. A. Blumenthal, and J. Kaplan. 1999. Impact of psychological factors on the pathogenesis of cardiovascular disease and implications for therapy. *Circulation* 99(16):2192–217.

Schoen, C., K. Davis, K. S. Collins, L. Greenberg, C. Des Roches, and M. Abrams. 1997. *The Commonwealth Fund Survey of the Health of Adolescent Girls.* November. New York: The Commonwealth Fund.

Seligman, M. E. P., and M. Csikszentmihalyi. 2000. Positive psychology: An introduction. *American Psychologist* 55(1):5–14.

Snyder, C. R., and S. J. Lopez, eds. 2002. *Handbook of Positive Psychology.* New York: Oxford University Press.

Tiller, W. A., R. McCraty, and M. Atkinson. 1996. Cardiac coherence: A new, noninvasive measure of autonomic nervous system order. *Alternative Therapies in Health and Medicine* 2(1):52–65.

Townsend, M. 2004. Stay calm everyone, there's Prozac in the drinking water. *Observer* (London), August 8.

Tsuji, H., F. J. Venditti Jr., E. S. Manders, J. C. Evans, M. G. Larson, C. L. Feldman, and D. Levy. 1994. Reduced heart rate variability and mortality risk in an elderly cohort. The Framingham Heart Study. *Circulation* 90(2):878–83.

Wang, J., H. Rao, G. S. Wetmore, P. M. Furlan, M. Korczykowski, D. F. Dinges, and J. A. Detre. 2005. Perfusion functional MRI reveals cerebral blood flow pattern under psychological stress. *Proceedings of the National Academy of Sciences USA* 102(49):17804–09.

Whooley, M. 2006. Depression and cardiovascular disease: Healing the broken-hearted. *Journal of the American Medical Association* 295(24):2874–81.

Doc Childre is the founder and chairman of the scientific advisory board of the Institute of HeartMath, the chairman of HeartMath, LLC, and the chairman and co-CEO of Quantum Intech. He is the author of eight books and a consultant to business leaders, scientists, educators, and the entertainment industry on Intui-Technology®. His HeartMath System and proprietary heart rhythm technology for coherence building, called the *Freeze-Framer*, have been reported on by Newsweek .com, *USA Today*, NBC-*Today Show*, ABC-*Good Morning America*, ABC *World News Tonight*, *CNN Headline News*, CNN.com, CNN Lou Dobbs, Wall Street Journal, *Harvard Business Review, The Economist's Intelligent Life, Business 2.0, Modern Health Care, Health Leaders, Prevention, Self, Natural Health, Alternative Medicine, Psychology Today, PGA.com, Golf magazine, Golf Illustrated, Allure, Cosmopolitan, FIRST for Women, Woman's World, New Woman, GQ Magazine, Men's Health, Men's Fitness, Los Angeles Times, San Francisco Chronicle, San Jose Mercury News*, and numerous other publications around the world.

Deborah Rozman, Ph.D., is a psychologist with thirty years of experience as a business executive, educator and author. She is President and co-CEO of Quantum Intech, overseeing strategic alliances and the expansion of HeartMath technologies worldwide. Quantum Intech develops and licenses health technologies and products powered by HeartMath that transform anxiety and improve health and performance. Deborah also serves on the Institute of HeartMath's scientific advisory board and Physics of Humanity council. She is a key spokesperson for the HeartMath system, giving media interviews and keynote addresses for executives, scientists, and health and technology companies throughout the world. She is listed in *Who's Who in California*.

more powerful HeartMath® tools for change
from new**harbinger**publications

TRANSFORMING ANGER
The HeartMath® Solution for Letting Go of Rage, Frustration, and Irritation

$12.95 • Item Code: 352X

TRANSFORMING ANXIETY
The HeartMath® Solution for Overcoming Fear and Worry and Creating Serenity

$12.95 • Item Code: 4445

TRANSFORMING STRESS
The HeartMath® Solution for Relieving Worry, Fatigue, and Tension

$12.95 • Item Code: 397X

DEPRESSED & ANXIOUS
The Dialectical Behavior Therapy Workbook for Overcoming Depression & Anxiety

$19.95 • Item Code: 3635

available from new**harbinger**publications
and fine booksellers everywhere

To order, call toll free **1-800-748-6273** or visit our online bookstore at **www.newharbinger.com**
(V, MC, AMEX • prices subject to change without notice)